HBR Guide to
Building Your
Business Case

Harvard Business Review Guides

Arm yourself with the advice you need to succeed on the job, from the most trusted brand in business. Packed with how-to essentials from leading experts, the HBR Guides provide smart answers to your most pressing work challenges.

The titles include:

HBR Guide to Better Business Writing

HBR Guide to Building Your Business Case

HBR Guide to Coaching Employees

HBR Guide to Finance Basics for Managers

HBR Guide to Getting the Mentoring You Need

HBR Guide to Getting the Right Job

HBR Guide to Getting the Right Work Done

HBR Guide to Giving Effective Feedback

HBR Guide to Leading Teams

HBR Guide to Making Every Meeting Matter

HBR Guide to Managing Stress at Work

HBR Guide to Managing Up and Across

HBR Guide to Negotiating

HBR Guide to Office Politics

HBR Guide to Persuasive Presentations

HBR Guide to Project Management

HBR Guide to
Building Your Business Case

Raymond Sheen

with **Amy Gallo**

HARVARD BUSINESS REVIEW PRESS

Boston, Massachusetts

The web addresses referenced in this book were live and correct at the time of the book's publication but may be subject to change.

Library of Congress Cataloging-in-Publication Data

Sheen, Raymond.
   HBR guide to building your business case / Raymond Sheen with Amy Gallo.
      pages cm. — (Hbr guide)
   ISBN 978-1-63369-002-8 (paperback)
   1. Business planning.   2. Strategic planning.   3. New business enterprises—Planning.   I. Gallo, Amy.   II. Title.
   HD30.28.S428 2015
   658.4'012—dc23

                                                        2015002965

The paper used in this publication meets the requirements of the American National Standard for Permanence of Paper for Publications and Documents in Libraries and Archives Z39.48–1992.

MIX
Paper from
responsible sources
FSC® C101537
www.fsc.org

What You'll Learn

You've got a great idea that will increase revenue or productivity—but how do you get approval to make it happen? By building a business case that clearly shows its value.

Maybe you struggle to win support for your projects because you're not sure what kind of data your stakeholders will trust, or naysayers tend to shoot down your ideas at the last minute. Perhaps you're intimidated by analysis and number crunching, so you just take a stab at estimating costs and benefits, with little confidence in your accuracy.

To get any idea off the ground in your company, you'll have to make a strong case for it. This guide gives you the tools to do that.

You'll get better at:

- Spelling out the business need for your idea

- Aligning your case with strategic goals

- Building the right team to shape and test your idea

- Calculating the return on investment

- Analyzing risks and opportunities

- Gaining support from colleagues

- Presenting your case to stakeholders

- Securing the resources your project needs

Contents

Introduction   xi

    Success is enabling a wise decision.

Section 1: PREPARE

1. **Know the Basics of Making a Case**   3

    You're telling a story about how to meet a business need.

2. **Learn How Your Company Evaluates Cases**   7

    Seek counsel from those who know what will fly.

Section 2: GET TO KNOW YOUR AUDIENCE

3. **Figure Out Who's Calling the Shots**   13

    Who really has the authority to give your project the green light?

4. **Understand Your Audience's Objectives**   17

    Find out what your stakeholders care about.

Section 3: BUILD THE CASE

5. Clarify the Need   25

   What pain are you trying to alleviate? What opportunity are you pursuing?

6. Build a Cross-Functional Team   33

   You need multiple perspectives to find the right solution.

7. Consider Alternatives   37

   The tough part is ruling out options.

8. Think Through the "How" at a High Level   43

   Pave the way for realistic estimates.

Section 4: CRUNCH THE NUMBERS

9. Estimate Costs and Benefits   49

   Peg them to categories in your company's P&L.

10. Calculate ROI   61

   Spreadsheets make it fairly painless.

11. Account for Risks   79

   Weigh the "what ifs."

Section 5: PRESENT YOUR CASE AND MOVE FORWARD

12. Prepare Your Document   87

   Summarize your story and support it with data.

13. Shop Your Case Around
93

Drum up support before decision time.

14. Are You Ready to Present?
97

Use this brief checklist to make sure you've covered all the bases.

15. Make Your Pitch
99

Appeal directly to decision makers.

16. Get to a Decision
105

"Yes" is meaningless unless stakeholders commit resources.

17. What Next?
109

Get started, even if it means heading back to the drawing board.

Appendix A: Avoid Common Mistakes
119

Appendix B: How to Give a Killer Presentation
123

BY CHRIS ANDERSON, TED CURATOR

Glossary
139

Index
143

About the Authors
149

Introduction

Whether you're pitching a new project at your company or seeking funds for a start-up, you'll need to develop a persuasive business case if you want your idea to go anywhere.

Your primary goal is to help people decide whether to invest resources in your idea. If you're making a case for a project or initiative within an organization, you're not starting in a vacuum. You have insight into your company's strategic priorities, and you probably know the people you're pitching to. But you've still got plenty of work to do. Your audience—the leaders of your unit or company—will expect you to put yourself in their shoes. (What are their chief concerns? How does your project address them?) They'll also expect a thoughtful analysis of the financials and the risks. They'll want to understand what impact your project will have on the P&L so they can intelligently weigh the costs and benefits.

How does that differ from pitching a start-up? As an entrepreneur, you're selling potential partners and funders on *you* as well as on your idea. Though that's an important distinction—it affects what you're trying to achieve and what you'll emphasize in your presentation—you'll take the same general approach you would inside an organization. In both situations, you must identify a clear business need, get to know your stakeholders, and tell them a compelling story about how to profitably meet that need.

That's what you'll learn to do in this guide. We'll focus on building internal business cases because that's the challenge most managers face—but the principles and tools will benefit entrepreneurs, too.

Internal business cases can serve many purposes, but here are three common reasons for developing one:

1. **You want to create a new product or service.** Here, your goal is to demonstrate the profits your offering would add to the bottom line. You'll help decision makers weigh sales estimates against the costs of development, manufacturing, and delivery.

2. **You want to invest in a large IT system.** When you're making a case for a new enterprise resource planning (ERP) system or a customer relationship management (CRM) database, for instance, you'll take into account the impact on the entire business—which departments will benefit and which will incur the costs.

3. **You want to improve your company's facilities.** This type of business case is becoming more common as organizations try to save money through energy efficiency. You may propose buying a

new building, for example, or remodeling an existing one.

You might also create a business case to prioritize projects and propose cutting a few; obtain additional resources for an ongoing initiative; invest in building a new capability; or decide whether to outsource a function.

Anytime you want your company to dedicate resources beyond what's already budgeted, you need to make a case. But you're not just doing legwork to persuade others to support your efforts. You're trying to figure out the best way to capture an opportunity or solve a problem. Developing a case will force you to generate and evaluate ideas in a disciplined way.

For that reason, success doesn't necessarily mean getting a "yes." It means enabling your leadership team to make a wise investment decision. A business case addresses the question "What happens if we take this course of action?" (*not* "Why is this a good idea?"). If the answer doesn't demonstrate that the benefits outweigh the costs or that the results align with the company's strategy, you haven't failed. On the contrary, you've saved your company from making a poor investment.

Let's look at a couple of fictional examples that make this point:

Jim, a brand manager, had an idea for a product that would help his midsize media company compete against larger rivals. His boss asked him to develop a business case, so Jim talked to customers, researched competitors, and looked at several alternatives. He worked with colleagues in finance, marketing, and sales to project revenues 10 years out and calculate ROI. His initial calculations showed promise for the new product. But his risk analysis revealed that if just one competitor got to market first, his company's market share would take a huge hit. During a quarterly review meeting with senior managers, Jim presented a well-researched, clearly articulated business case that incorporated both his original estimates and a worst-case scenario. They said the product looked like a good opportunity, but they agreed with Jim that it felt too risky, so they didn't fund it.

Now consider Catherine, a VP of IT at a manufacturing firm. Her boss asked her to put together a business case for a new inventory-management system. The managers of the company's six plants had been clamoring for this for more than a year, saying that they didn't have enough visibility into one another's inventory levels. Catherine traveled to the plants to learn more about what each one needed the new system to do. She then met with several vendors to review off-the-shelf options and discuss what customization might be required. After getting rough cost estimates, she worked with each plant manager to project how much the new system would speed up fulfillment times and then calculated the savings over the next five years. She presented a well-researched, clearly articulated business case to the CFO, the CEO, and her boss, the CIO. They gave her approval to select a vendor, develop an implementation plan, and cost out the system in detail.

So, who did a better job—Jim or Catherine? You might be tempted to say Catherine, because her project won approval and moved to the next stage. But ultimately, *both* succeeded. They both helped senior managers make an informed decision. Not gaining support for a project after you've devoted time and energy to it is never fun. But as long as you've presented a well-constructed business case, it's OK—and sometimes desirable—to get a "no" from the powers that be. Even if you've persuaded senior managers *not* to approve your project, you'll have earned their trust by showing how carefully you've thought it through. The first step in helping your company decide whether or not to invest in your idea is understanding what goes into a business case.

Section 1
Prepare

Chapter 1
Know the Basics
of Making a Case

No matter where you work or what type of idea you're pitching, you should follow the same basic process for any business case you develop. I'll briefly outline it here to give you a sense of the whole before delving into the individual steps in later chapters.

Here, in section 1, "Prepare," you learn how to put yourself in the right frame of mind. Don't even think about constructing a logical argument yet or wrestling with the numbers—it's much too soon for that level of detail. Instead, imagine you're telling a story.

The story starts, as all good ones do, with a problem. This is the *business need* you're trying to solve. For example: Are customers complaining about a particular product feature? Is finance struggling to produce accurate reports because of an outdated IT system? Has your company lost market share to a competitor that's offering adjacent services?

You may spot the need yourself. Or your manager may ask you to address a concern that came up during a strategic-planning discussion or a product-line review. Once you've pinpointed the problem or opportunity, it's time to identify your story's characters:

- Your *stakeholders* have the authority to approve or reject your business case. They might include your boss, your boss's boss, or your company's senior leadership team (section 2, "Get to Know Your Audience").

- *Beneficiaries* are those who stand to gain from what you're proposing. You'll usually have more than one group to consider, either inside or outside the organization. If you're recommending a new IT system for the finance department, you'll have two sets of beneficiaries: the people who run the financial reports and those who receive them.

- You'll draw on *subject-matter experts* to create the case. They're the people with insight into what it will take to solve the problem. If you're proposing a new product, you'll probably pull in colleagues from R&D, sales, and marketing. For any type of project, you'll work closely with finance to come up with cost estimates.

Then you'll consider alternatives for meeting the business need—different ways your story might play out (section 3, "Build the Case"). With the experts you've brought in, you'll explore several options: Which is the most efficient? The most cost-effective? The most appropriate for the organization's culture and capabilities?

After making the best choice in light of what you know at that point, you'll create a very high-level project plan to roughly gauge the amount of time and resources you'll need and the value your solution will bring. Estimating costs and benefits can be daunting for managers who are new to developing business cases. But as you'll see in section 4, "Crunch the Numbers," it's pretty straightforward if you've got the rest of your story clearly laid out: your business need, the alternatives you've considered, and your recommended approach to meeting the need.

You'll enter those numbers into a spreadsheet to determine the return on investment (ROI). A classic ROI calculation (benefits divided by cost) is static—it provides a snapshot of one point in time—so very few companies still rely on it alone. It's better to use a more nuanced version of ROI and look at a stream of costs and benefits over months or years by examining the break-even point, payback period, net present value, or internal rate of return—or some combination of those measures (which we'll cover in chapter 10).

Finally, it's time to tell your story. Package it in whatever format your company uses for business cases and present it to your stakeholders. If no templates exist, create your own logical format (you'll find suggestions and samples in section 5, "Present Your Case and Move Forward"). Above all else, your story needs to be clear—it should *not* be a mystery. Your stakeholders won't be receptive if they have to puzzle out which solution you're recommending, what divisions it will affect, or what it will cost.

Whether you get a yea or nay on your business case, you're not done, so chapter 17, "What Next?" will walk you through the first few steps. If your case is approved, you'll kick off your project and get started. If it's not approved, you still have work to do, such as wrapping things up so you can easily dust off your business case in the future if need be.

Knowing the basic components of a business case will help you get into the right frame of mind to gather, polish, and present your compelling story. But before you dive into the work, you need to know what the decision makers look for in a business case.

Chapter 2
Learn How Your Company Evaluates Cases

How you tell the story of your business case depends on how your organization reviews and approves projects and initiatives.

To figure that out, you need to answer questions such as:

- Does your company have a formal process for evaluating cases? If so, what's involved—and is it connected to other processes, such as the budget review cycle?

- Does your company review cases as they come up, or at specific times tied to your fiscal year or budgeting season?

- Do stakeholders look at projects individually or as a portfolio?

- What level of detail will your audience want? For instance, are they looking for sales projections by region, product line, year, or a combination of the three?

- Does the organization approve entire projects at once or in discrete phases?

Find out as much as you can from a colleague who knows the ins and outs of the process. Reach out to your boss and members of your internal network to connect you with someone who's made a successful pitch. What forms should you use? Which decision makers should you talk to in advance? What types of projects typically get approved?

Large companies like GE, where I spent several years on the corporate staff, usually have a formal process with preset templates. And they typically review business cases at specific times during the year. Some other companies I've worked with do it as part of their annual budgeting process: Senior leaders look at a portfolio of 20 to 30 cases at a time and decide which to fund with the budget that's available. Say they've got $10 million to work with. After reviewing the company's strategic priorities, they may decide to spend roughly $5 million on product development; for instance, $3 million on compliance projects and $2 million on cost-reduction projects. They'll evaluate the portfolio against those numbers and do the necessary juggling to hit them. Companies that review business cases annually often set aside a small portion of the budget for off-cycle opportunities that pop up throughout the year.

Many large companies also have a *tollgate process*. That means a project lead prepares a business case for an initial discovery phase—not for the entire project. If stakeholders give that a green light, they'll ask the team to break the rest of the project into phases (such as design, development, testing, and commercialization, if you're proposing a new product) and to return for approvals along the way. This allows senior managers to hedge their bets, committing more resources only as it becomes clearer that the benefits will outweigh the costs.

Though they sometimes have less structure, smaller organizations work similarly. They may have set times to review cases, for example, and approve initial phases before committing to an entire project.

One small internet service provider I worked with reviewed its business cases at a monthly leadership meeting. After going over the previous month's sales and costs, senior managers would discuss which new projects to fund. Another company—an automotive supplier—developed business cases before responding to requests for proposals (RFPs). That exercise helped stakeholders decide whether to bid on new-vehicle projects and how aggressive their bids should be.

Regardless of company size, you'll need to know who has the authority to approve or reject your case. In some organizations, even small projects require approval by senior leaders. The decisions may be made at the functional, unit, or regional level.

If your organization doesn't dictate a process for business cases or you're requesting resources during an off-cycle time, find out what others have done to get approval. Ask around to see which colleagues have a track record of success and request meetings with them to learn what materials they used, whose help they enlisted, what twists and turns they encountered, and what mistakes they're now careful not to repeat.

Knowing what's worked—and what hasn't—is the best way to develop a case that stands a chance of being approved. We'll dig into learning more about strategic priorities and figuring out who has the authority to approve your case in the next section.

Section 2
Get to Know Your Audience

Chapter 3
Figure Out Who's Calling the Shots

The fate of your project or initiative will usually lie with a small group or even one individual.

Early on, ask your boss who will be evaluating your idea so you can build a case that speaks to their priorities (see chapter 4, "Understand Your Audience's Objectives"). Maybe it's your boss's boss or the division head. Or perhaps the review committee consists of eight leaders representing different parts of the organization—and they take a vote on every idea presented.

Knowing which people will review your business case isn't the same as understanding who makes the final decision. At one company I worked with, a committee of six executives looked at cases during the annual budget meeting. But everyone knew that the CFO had the last word.

It's not always clear who's calling the shots, but you can get important clues by looking at business cases that have been approved. If projects that benefit marketing often get a green light, some decision-making power may lie with the CMO. If cases from HR and finance tend to sail through, the heads of those departments may have a large say in what gets approved.

Once you've figured out who has decision rights, how do you appeal to that person or group? By finding sources of influence and support.

Who Has Influence?

In most organizations, there's a dominant department— and its leader wields informal authority, regardless of his title. At P&G, marketing is king. At GE, it's finance. And at General Motors, it's manufacturing. You can assume that the dominant department's objectives will trump others when decision makers review business cases.

Which area of your company has that kind of power? Projects under its purview stand the best chance of approval, especially in a close race for resources. At P&G, leaders reviewing cases will ask "Which projects promise the most market growth?" At GE, "Which ones will give us the best financial returns?" At General Motors, "Which ones will make our plants most efficient?" Identify your company's dominant department—and cast your idea in light of its goals.

Who Will Have Your Back?

Finding a champion on the review committee—or one who's close to it—will help you get a fair review, because she will lobby on behalf of your case. But how do you find a project champion?

Look at each member of the review committee: Whose goals and concerns will your project address most directly? That person is a potential champion. Reach out and ask what her department is trying to achieve in the coming year. Get a sense of what big projects are under way and which need more support. Explain how your initiative can help fill in gaps or address trouble spots. This is a time when your personal network will pay dividends. Work with people you know in that department or division to clarify the problem or business need that your project will address. Ask them specifically what the champion will care most about and how to address those concerns. Then, ask your contacts to introduce you to the potential champion or to set up a meeting so you can clarify the need and explain your ideas. Even if you've never met the potential champion, you're more likely to get her ear since you're working on a problem that affects her division. If she is interested, ask her to review your business case when it's ready and champion it within the review committee. You'll also want to keep her informed and use her as a sounding board along the way.

Of course, having someone influential on your side does little good if you don't have a strong case that meets a business need and well-thought-out financials. If those elements are missing, even a powerful champion can't help you. So now that you've won over one person, it's time to tailor your pitch to meet the objectives of the organization and the broader committee.

Chapter 4
Understand Your Audience's Objectives

Once you know who the decision makers are, the next step is to discover what they care about most. Senior leaders are looking for projects and initiatives that fit the company's strategy, and they're likely to reject those that don't.

But many managers don't understand that, so they have trouble getting even solid business cases approved. They believe that the benefits are obvious—and neglect to align their cases with broader objectives.

Very few organizations have money or people sitting around waiting to be deployed. So when you're making a business case, you're inevitably competing with others for limited resources. The best way to come out on top is to explicitly demonstrate how your idea supports the company's priorities.

GETTING TO KNOW POTENTIAL INVESTORS OR PARTNERS

If you're an entrepreneur developing a business case, it can be tough to unearth your audience's objectives. After all, you may not know the people you're pitching to. But with a little creativity, you can get the information.

Find other entrepreneurs who have worked with your audience. Sometimes investors will offer this information if asked; otherwise, you may need to tap your network to see if anyone knows whom else they've funded.

Reach out to these fellow entrepreneurs through LinkedIn, Twitter, or mutual acquaintances to get the inside scoop. And don't just ask about your audience's business priorities. You also want to understand what they're passionate about and tailor your business case to that. They're more likely to invest in or partner with you if they have an emotional connection to your project, in addition to confidence in the financials.

If you're not entirely sure what those are, look at the annual report, the CEO's letter to shareholders, and all-staff memos. Consider: What are we trying to do this year overall? Are we in growth mode or cutting costs? Are we attempting to go global quickly or focusing on one or two regions? As you comb through those external and internal communications, you'll probably find a few main themes. Typically, the people evaluating your business case are also charged with meeting those larger objectives—and they'll want to understand how your idea helps them do that. If your executive team has set a goal of 5% top-line growth, demonstrate how your project will add directly to revenue. If you can't do that, highlight metrics that show an indirect connection: Will your idea reduce the time to market by 3%? Will it save cycle time? Whatever the benefits, clearly explain how they relate to overarching goals.

That strategy paid off for one utility company I worked with. Several years ago, market research firm J.D. Power evaluated customer satisfaction at 300 utility companies. The company I worked with came in dead last. Worst in the nation. For the next two years, the executive committee set its sights on reversing that dismal rating, approving any solid business case that dealt with the problem. If you couldn't make a case for improving customer satisfaction in some way, it didn't matter how much money your project would save the company or how much growth it would generate—you'd get turned down. Five years later, when J.D. Power did a follow-up study, the company scored in the top 50% on customer satisfaction—a huge improvement.

Even if your company's goals are that narrowly defined, your stakeholders may not agree on how to achieve them, so you have to understand each decision maker's perspective on execution. Say your organization is keen to reduce costs. The CFO may feel the best way to do that is to streamline manufacturing processes, but the COO may advocate outsourcing.

That's one reason it's critical to pull in experts from various functions to help you build your business case (see chapter 6, "Build a Cross-Functional Team," for more on this). They'll shed light on what their department's leaders care about. For example, someone from finance can probably give you insight into what the CFO thinks about the company's strategic goals and how to achieve them.

How else can you get the information you need about your audience?

1. **Gather intelligence from above.** In addition to tapping cross-functional experts, ask your boss about your stakeholders' priorities, values, goals, and decision-making styles. What might they gain or lose from the opportunity you're presenting? How are they influenced? Do they like to be presented with strong opinions supported by facts, or do they prefer to go through the thinking process with you and then reach their own conclusions? How do they like to receive information? Are they numbers oriented? Customer focused?

   Your champion can be a good source of intelligence, too. Ask her the same questions. In addition, inquire about anything you *shouldn't* include in the proposal because it might push the buttons of one of the decision makers.

   If you have direct access to stakeholders, approach them with three simple questions: What are your group's chief objectives this year? How do you measure success? What are your barriers? Then use their answers to inform your case. If they're struggling to respond to increasingly stringent environmental protection regulations, for example, highlight how your idea will help them do that.

2. **Examine your stakeholders' track records.** Look at the projects they've approved over the past two years. What do they have in common? Do they all focus on improving customer satisfaction? Lowering costs? Growing your product line? Finding new sources of revenue? Adding capabilities? Now look at projects your stakeholders have killed—they, too, may have telling similarities. Of course, it's important to put those approvals and rejections in context. If your company just acquired a business or went through a restructuring, the goals may have changed.

As you're digging for insights into your stakeholders, also consider what *their* stakeholders care about. Even if the people reviewing your business case have decision-making authority, they'll have to justify their choices when actual revenues and costs start rolling in. So think carefully about your audience's audience: If you pitch to the CEO, he'll probably try to anticipate the board of directors' reactions and concerns. A marketing VP will channel the CMO. Put yourself in your stakeholders' shoes and give them what they'll need to convey the value of your idea to those above them.

Now that you know what your audience cares about most, you can turn to gathering the specific information you need, starting with the pain point or opportunity you've identified.

Section 3
Build the Case

Chapter 5
Clarify the Need

You can't build your team, brainstorm solutions, or crunch the numbers until the business need is crystal clear.

Try thinking of it as a pain point: Plant managers don't have an effective way to share performance information. The sales force in Europe is losing bids because of a new competitor. Whatever the pain, that's the source of the need, and your task is to figure out how to alleviate the suffering.

Of course, some projects are driven by opportunities, not by urgent problems. Your company might save 40% in operating costs by switching to a new CRM system, for example, or become eligible for $2 million in tax incentives by updating its wastewater treatment facility by year-end.

You may identify the pain point or opportunity yourself—maybe you have an idea about how to remedy a product defect or make a process more efficient. But more often, stakeholders will hand you a problem and say, "Fix this," or point to an opportunity and say, "Check this out." In either situation, research the business need so you'll have a thorough understanding of it.

Let's look at an example that shows how you might do this.

Imagine that a manufacturing VP comes to a strategic-planning meeting and says, "We can't meet our goals this year if we don't fix or replace our inventory system. Our counts are all wrong. In some places, we have excess; in others, we keep running out." The CEO asks you, an IT manager, to look into it. Now it's your responsibility to build a case for investing in a new system, or not, depending on what you find.

Your primary challenge at this point? Learn *why* the inventory levels are off and which parts of the business suffer as a result. Here are the steps you'll take.

Talk to Beneficiaries

First, ask the manufacturing people who use the current system what they think is going on: When did the problem start? How does it manifest itself? How often? How does the problem prevent their teams from doing their work effectively? Who else in the company does it affect? Talk to those individuals as well, and gather relevant data, reports, surveys—whatever evidence your beneficiaries can provide. If possible, observe the issue firsthand. You might visit plants and watch how inventory is captured and entered into the system. You could shadow the people who use the system and observe how they complete their tasks.

Your job is to listen *and* probe further. The beneficiaries may not know the underlying reason for the problem: "We're not sure why the inventories keep showing up wrong. But when we go to the warehouse floor, the count is always off." It's up to you to discover the cause and identify a reasonable solution.

The beneficiaries may have a solution in mind. (Perhaps the manufacturing VP learned about an inventory management system that he believes will provide a more accurate count.) But sometimes what they want isn't the best fix. Of course you need to look into this option, but it might not be your final recommendation, especially if it's costly or difficult to adopt.

Analyze Processes

Next, examine the problem yourself. Don't just take people's word for it. Use a process-flow analysis—a visual representation of the various stages. Through conversations with beneficiaries and your own observations, develop a full picture of how inventory moves and where amounts are captured. Lay out all the steps of the inventory flow, illustrating how they connect and noting decision points (for example, who decides when to enter amounts into the system?). This is critical because you may find out that it isn't an IT problem at all. Maybe there's a training issue or a communication breakdown in the supply chain. You could discover places where the process falls apart.

Look at the sample flowchart in figure 5-1. Note how many parts of the process depend on manual updates

FIGURE 5-1

Process-flow analysis

By creating a visual process map like this sample flowchart, you'll develop a more complete picture of the business need you're trying to address.

Inventory management process

1. Order parts
Quantity ordered based on forecasted need and inventory recorded in system.

2. Receive parts
Quantity checked against order. Mismatch requires manual correction in the system.

3. Send parts to stockroom
Quantity not checked when stockroom shelves parts.

4. Schedule kits
Kits scheduled based on parts quantities in system. If counts are low, system automatically generates new orders. Inaccurate counts in system lead to too many or too few parts ordered.

5. Pull parts for kits
Stockroom manually pulls parts for kits, and system automatically subtracts inventory. If stockroom is short, system requires manual parts order. If stockroom finds a defective part, it's sent to QC—but quantity in system doesn't change unless QC scraps the part, which may take weeks.

6. Assemble kits
Kit quantity checked by operator during assembly. If short, part requested from stockroom and count manually updated in system. Extra parts sometimes returned to stockroom, sometimes scrapped.

—we've got lots of room for human error. And the lag time after quality control identifies a defective part makes it even harder for the inventory system to reflect accurate counts. You'll want to examine all these pain points to fully expose the need.

Agree on What the Solution Should Accomplish

Once you've gathered all this information and formed a clearer picture of the business need, go back to your stakeholders (the CEO and the manufacturing VP) and make sure your assumptions match theirs about what the solution should do and what the constraints are. For example, a new inventory system may need to work in Europe as well as in the United States—that's an assumption you'll want to confirm with your stakeholders, even if it seems obvious to you. Constraints might include compatibility with other IT systems or short windows of time when the rollout can take place. Use the following questions to guide the discussion with your stakeholders:

- Where will the solution be used? In what offices or facilities? In how many countries?

- Who will be affected by the solution? A single department or the entire organization?

- How quickly does the solution need to be in place? Will we roll it out over time or all at once?

- How should we measure the solution's effectiveness? Do we have a baseline that we can compare against?

TESTING THE NEED WITH A STEALTH PROJECT

What if you *suspect* a market need but lack data to back it up? Or senior managers don't want to alter a product, despite customer complaints? Or they tend to reject out-of-the-mainstream ideas like yours?

Try demonstrating the importance of your business case—to yourself and others—by doing a stealth project as proof of concept. A small pilot project can help you test your hypothesis about the need before you develop and present a solution.

Take this example: At GE, we had some problems with a product that my engineering team was responsible for. We thought fixing them would require a time-consuming, expensive redesign, but then one of my engineers suggested a minor change in the manufacturing process. Not everyone agreed it would work, so he and the manufacturing manager pulled operators aside and asked them to collect product and process data over

---

- Should we combine the solution with another related initiative?

Stakeholders may not have the answers to all these questions, or they may ask you to make recommendations. When that happens, it usually means there's no constraint with respect to that question, which is helpful to know.

a two-week period. The data demonstrated the validity of his idea, and he got approval for it.

The stealth approach has its risks, of course. You might annoy people or even get into trouble, particularly if you're spending funds meant for other projects. Doing a proof of concept without getting approval can also signal to senior managers that you don't trust them to make smart decisions.

To reduce these risks, keep your project lean and focused—and frame it as a fact-finding experiment.

Know what you want to learn, and spend only as much money as it takes to do that. Get your answer and move on. Don't let the project carry on for months. And document everything you learn so you can include your findings in your business case.

You may discover that the business need isn't so great, after all—so be prepared to abandon your idea.

Document, Document, Document

Record everything you learn: where the pain comes from, who's experiencing it, and what the solution needs to accomplish. This documentation will save you time later as you prepare your presentation to stakeholders—they'll want to see what you're basing your recommendations on (see Section 5, "Present Your Case and Move Forward").

The process can be as straightforward as jotting down notes or entering them in an Excel or PowerPoint file—or you might use your company's project management software to log evidence of the need. Keep track of who told you what. That way, you can go back for clarification in the likely event that you receive conflicting or partial information from beneficiaries. This will also help you refer stakeholders' questions to the right people.

After doing all this work, what if you find out the business need isn't strong? That's OK. You're still helping your stakeholders make an informed decision about whether to invest, and how much. This is a good time to meet with your champion and ask for guidance. Should you continue to develop a business case even though there isn't much benefit? Is there an additional benefit that you haven't considered that should be added to the business case? For instance, you may find that a new inventory system will speed up delivery time by just 5%—and that the project won't generate any return for several years, given software and innovation costs. But stakeholders may still want to go ahead if the new system brings manufacturing up-to-date with competitors. When I sat on the review committee at a medical device company, we saw many projects that didn't immediately deliver huge revenues or cost savings. Still, they had to get done—sometimes to comply with new FDA guidelines, sometimes to address concerns of key hospitals or doctors and gain their support for new products.

Figuring out the specifics of how to address the business need and with what resources can be a daunting task. Fortunately, you don't typically have to go it alone. Your next step is to gather a team of internal experts who can help you get the information you need.

Chapter 6
Build a Cross-Functional Team

Unless you're an entrepreneur, you probably won't build the business case on your own. Inside established companies, it's a team effort. Both beneficiaries and subject-matter experts will help you determine which solution to the underlying problem will work best, how much it will cost, how much revenue it will bring in, and so on.

You probably won't have a full-time, dedicated team at your disposal. Instead, you'll bring people together from various departments at different points in the process—when it's time to brainstorm alternatives, for instance, or estimate the costs and benefits.

Building a cross-functional team allows you to examine solutions from multiple angles. Otherwise, you'll develop the case from a particular point of view—most likely your department's—and run the risk of overlooking an option or important costs and benefits.

Include the following types of team members:

- **A finance representative.** Too many people assume that finance is the enemy. This couldn't be further from the truth, especially when you're developing a business case. Someone from finance can establish current costs and benefits, and make accurate projections. And the earlier you bring in this person, the better. Don't attempt to do the forecasting and ROI calculations on your own, even if you're good with numbers. You might make incorrect assumptions about industry dynamics, depreciation, personnel costs, and so on without guidance from someone with a big-picture view of the company's revenues and expenses.

- **Beneficiaries.** If you're proposing a product fix, engineering may be your primary internal beneficiary, but salespeople could also gain an advantage. So include someone from each group. Don't overemphasize the role of your beneficiaries— since they're the ones feeling the pain, they're not going to be your most objective problem solvers. But ask them to voice their chief concerns as the team identifies and weighs solutions, just as they did when they helped you gain a deeper understanding of the business need.

- **Someone who regularly talks with customers.** If customers feel the pain most acutely, or the proposed solution will affect them in any way (most new ideas do), consult with someone who knows what they care about—or who can ask them. This may be an account manager, a customer service rep, or a marketing associate who conducts customer surveys.

- **External experts.** You might not get all the information and insight you need in-house. If your company has never solved this kind of problem before, ask outside experts for their recommendations. Considering a new ERP system? Reach out to your network of IT professionals, online communities, vendors, and partners. Find out what they use and how well it's working for them.

What might a team that includes all those members look like? Let's return to the inventory problem we looked at in chapter 5, "Clarify the Need." You'd want to bring in people most affected by the incorrect counts: several manufacturing representatives (from different plants), colleagues from finance and sales, and someone who can speak to the concerns of suppliers. You could also consult with vendors who sell inventory systems to find out what additional features the latest software provides.

By involving these people in building the business case, you don't just gain access to information (though that's important); you also gain their *support*. They're engaged, right along with you, in finding the right solution. And it's much easier to get approval if your stakeholders know that people from their departments helped create the proposal.

Once you know what types of team members you need, handpick individuals you work well with—those who will be generous with their time and information. You can add occasional "guest stars" to the lineup. For instance, if you're bringing the team together to brainstorm solutions, include people who thrive in meetings like that—creative colleagues who are quick on their feet, not black-and-white thinkers wedded to their own ideas.

But keep the core group small—no more than six people, if possible. You'd lose momentum and focus if you spent weeks or months consulting everyone who knows something about the problem. You want a tight team of experts who can efficiently help you work out the best solution.

Even with a dream team, it's rare you'll come up with the best solution out of the gate. That's because there's rarely one solution to any given problem. You'll need to generate and weigh several alternatives.

Chapter 7
Consider Alternatives

Now that you've selected your team, it's time to start brainstorming. Bring your experts and beneficiaries together to think about potential solutions. Briefly describe the pain, who's feeling it, and its underlying cause—just to orient the group—and ask for suggestions on how to alleviate it. Lay out the ideas that stakeholders or beneficiaries proposed early on, and ask your team to generate several more. Encourage people to look beyond their own unit or function: How have other departments met this need? What have other companies done? What's worked, and what hasn't?

At the beginning of a meeting like this, don't put constraints on people. Let them think out loud. Then, after the team generates options, you can mention limitations to focus their thinking and spur additional ideas: Remind people that the solution can't involve relocating staff, for instance, or that it must take into account the products the company will launch in the coming year.

Open the floor to any and all ideas for solving the problem with the following guidelines in mind.

Forgo Precision—and Push Beyond the Obvious

Generate alternatives quickly. You aren't drafting project plans or identifying specific vendors or product names. Instead, you're coming up with a generic system, initiative, or product to recommend. Don't get hung up on particulars. If your team starts laying out specifications for a solution, pull them back to the big picture. You'll gather basic specs later, after you've narrowed down your options and begun assessing them. And once you get approval, you'll have time to sort out the nitty-gritty details. The goal right now is to sketch out several directions you might take, not to pave the actual path.

Often there's a front-runner idea from the very beginning—perhaps a solution suggested by your champion or adopted by leaders in your industry. Don't fixate on this option, even if it's the CEO's idea. Stakeholders will expect you to seriously consider multiple options. After all, they want to see that you've conducted a thorough analysis, not just gone with the obvious solution.

If you struggle to come up with other options, try these techniques to broaden your perspective:

- **Start with the desired end state.** Look at how other organizations have achieved the business performance you're aiming for, whether it's faster time to market or improved quality. Would those approaches work for your company?

- **Think about how other departments would address the issue.** What would the project look like if IT took the lead? How about sales? HR? Engineering? Supply chain?

- **Consider how you'd do the project with different constraints.** What if you had twice the time to complete the project? Or half the time? What would change if you outsourced (or insourced) the work? What if you had to scale the solution to do the same thing 100 times?

Consider a Do-Nothing Option

A business case addresses the question "What happens if we take this course of action?" But you also need to consider the consequences of doing nothing. That will help you articulate the business need when you present your case. For example: "If we stick with our current line, sales will continue to drop 10% a year. This new product will reverse that trend—in fact, we project a 20% increase in sales over the next five years."

Sometimes doing nothing is a viable option. That's often true of internal improvement projects. Suppose the supply chain organization wants to modify its parts-traceability program to meet the industry standard. The manager developing the business case will include a do-nothing option to show stakeholders what costs they'll avoid by approving the project. She'll answer questions along these lines: "If we don't get in line with the industry standard, what work-arounds will we need in order to keep selling our products? Will we lose any customers?" If the do-nothing costs aren't prohibitive, stakeholders may decide to absorb them rather than invest in changing the program.

Narrow Down Your Possibilities

When I reviewed business cases at GE, I didn't like being given one option and told that was the way we had to do it. Nor did I want someone to walk me through 25 alternatives. Chances are your review committee members are looking for the same thoughtful balance. Present stakeholders with two or three reasonable choices. This means you need to whittle down the list from your brainstorming session. Questions like these will help:

- Which option costs the least?

- Which is the fastest to implement?

- Which has the fewest risks?

- Which brings in the most revenue?

Often, one option will meet several of those conditions—but each idea you present should have at least one big thing going for it. Don't offer an obviously unacceptable solution in contrast to your preferred choice. It will appear that you're trying to manipulate the review board.

Once you've selected a few options, talk with the champion you identified early on—ask her what she thinks of your alternatives and which ones stand the best chance of approval. Also, review the options with your subject-matter experts. If there is something in an option that is impossible or unacceptable, modify the option or drop it. For instance, if one option violates existing codes or standards, revise it to make it compliant.

When you prepare the financials, one of your options may stand out as a clear winner. So you'll present it to the review committee—but also share other options you considered. If you looked at three alternatives but immediately saw that two would generate no revenue growth (or would cost too much, or present a compliance problem), explain that in your presentation. Stakeholders expect to see which viable choices you rejected and on what grounds.

You have several good ideas for solving the problem, but that's only half the work. Now it's time to dig a bit deeper and consider what it would mean to implement them.

Chapter 8
Think Through the "How" at a High Level

To build a strong case, you'll need to paint a picture—in very broad strokes—of how the organization would implement the solution you're proposing. You're not doing a detailed project plan at this point. Far from it. You're just sketching a basic outline of what the project requires so your estimates of costs and benefits will be realistic.

This helps you see more clearly whose support you'll need. If you start to think through the "how" and suddenly realize that marketing and sales will have to contribute resources, you'll need to tap them for information when you're working on the financials and get their buy-in before you present the case.

This process also reveals transition costs, which many managers overlook (see chapter 9, "Estimate Costs and Benefits"). They're often so gung ho about their pet solution that they forget to consider how they're going to migrate the company's data into that fancy new system, how they'll train everyone to use it, or how they'll shut down and archive the old system. To get the fullest picture of what implementation will mean to your project, you'll need to work with your team to get their feedback and to set a rough plan.

Consult Your Team

Here again, you'll bring in your subject-matter experts to get their input on various practical questions. For example:

- What work must be done before the company can switch to the new system?

- Who needs to do it?

- What—and whom—will the actual switch involve?

- Where will major costs be incurred before, during, and after the switch?

- Will we roll out the system once companywide or multiple times for different customers, departments, or locations?

- What training will employees need?

- What systems, products, or processes will be eliminated when this new system is implemented?

Beneficiaries will have strong opinions on how to implement the solution since they're often the ones who will do the work. They may believe the system needs to be rolled out across the organization all at once. Or they may think that their department should be responsible for managing the project. Make sure your case reflects their input so you'll have their buy-in when it's time for them to contribute. Let's say you're proposing to develop a new product for the Asian market. The marketing and sales force in Asia may think that they should manage the project. If your recommendation is that the project will be managed by the R&D department in Germany, you might add that a person from the Asian marketing team will relocate to Germany or that the prototype reviews and design reviews will be done in Hong Kong. That way, the team in Asia won't stand in your way when it's time to roll out the project.

Make the Plan Directionally Correct

You're still not at the point where you need a detailed project plan, so don't go too far into the weeds. But you'll want to figure out, for instance, whether you'll use the new system in three countries or five. You can think later about which country you'll do first, and so on, depending on what's happening in those markets. For now, just knowing the "where" at a high level will help you consider what kind of work will go into getting the system ready (translating it into three or five languages, testing it with user groups in each country, and so on). You're not sorting out every task—just the types of tasks and the people involved.

As you do this, you may realize that one or more of your alternatives aren't feasible, after all. Perhaps you discover a large hidden cost or see that one of the solutions, when implemented, would violate a stated constraint. In that case, go back to your team of experts to reconsider other options or generate new ones.

With the key issues identified and your rough plan mapped out, you're ready to turn to the financials.

Section 4
Crunch the Numbers

Chapter 9
Estimate Costs and Benefits

Before you calculate the ROI, you'll need a more accurate projection of costs and benefits. For many people (especially nontechnical folks), working with these numbers can be intimidating. But now that you've identified and clarified the business need, gathered the right team, and tested your assumptions, this part won't be hard.

Start by estimating costs and benefits for the option that you and your team consider to be the most viable. Once you've done that, explore the alternatives by adjusting the numbers. Will they cost more to implement? Will they return revenue sooner? Usually you'll change just a few figures. For example, one option may be to do a phased rollout instead of a universal launch. Your project costs are likely to be similar, but some of your benefits won't show up until later—so you'll decrease those numbers for the first year or two.

Stick to two or three alternatives. You'll drive yourself—and your team—crazy if you explore all the possibilities available to you. On rare occasions, you may need to develop a full-blown case for more than one alternative. For example, in a financial services company I worked with, some executives wanted to outsource the call center; others pushed to keep it in-house and update the antiquated system. We knew the review team had advocates on both sides, so we had to create two separate cases— one to outsource, one to upgrade—for equal consideration. In this case, the outsourcing option had a faster payback, but ultimately did not deliver as much value to the company. The organization decided to upgrade the existing system. This option cost more and took longer, but it also created a long-term capability that grew in value over time.

Exceptions like this aside, once you have your alternatives identified, you'll want to assemble the figures that will be most useful in helping your stakeholders make a solid decision.

The Numbers You Need

Base your estimates on the categories in your company's income statement (P&L)—those are the numbers your reviewers will care about. Together, your costs and benefits make up the cash flow for your project. Consider when they'll begin and how they'll change over time. Don't look at the total pot of money your company will "net" at the end of five or ten years. Instead, show a stream of expenses and income: Generate estimates for each year until the benefits run out.

How many years out do you go? It depends on the project. Your company may have guidelines—or your stakeholders may have a preference. But if not, follow these rules of thumb: For IT projects, estimate three to five years of cash flows. (After that, most IT systems become obsolete.) For product development cases, look at the product life cycle. In some industries, such as consumer electronics, that's three years. In others, like the aircraft industry, it's 15. Facilities projects usually need a minimum of 15 years.

With those rough guidelines in mind, gather the cost and benefit information.

Costs

You'll look at two main types of costs. The first type, *project costs,* consists of project expenditures and capital expenditures. Project expenditures usually occur at the beginning—they tend to include development, testing and qualification, training and deployment, and travel costs. They're pretty straightforward to estimate: You consider the type of work to be done on the project and approximately how long it will take, and then put together your estimate for completing that work. I generally start by assessing how many people I need on the team and, using an average salary rate, I can project the personnel costs. Then I do a rough estimate of travel and supplies to be purchased on the project.

Capital expenditures aren't as simple. A project cost becomes a capital expenditure when you've spent the money to acquire or develop an asset. Anything that is capitalized must be depreciated—which means finance must show the decrease in value over the asset's life. On your project ROI calculation, you can record the cost of an asset as a single number, under the year the company acquired the asset, or you can spread the cost over the years it's depreciated. (Either way, you capture the total cost.) Check with your finance person to find out how you must represent the costs in your analysis. The financial rules for capital expenditures are complex, and they often change, so you'll want expert guidance.

The second type of costs, *operating costs,* can be tricky because you're estimating how much money it will take to maintain whatever you're proposing. These include overhead—costs, such as personnel, office space, maintenance and licensing fees, and any other ongoing expenses. Consider: Will you need a part-time staff member to monitor your new centralized procurement system? Or will your new product require a dedicated sales team that understands its technical features? What about changes to the help desk? Some projects will reduce operating costs, so look at expenses you'll eliminate as well as those you'll add.

The department doing the project work incurs the project costs (IT, if it's creating a new customer management system). By contrast, operating costs can crop up anywhere in the business (for instance, in the departments that will use the system).

As discussed in chapter 8, "Think Through the 'How' at a High Level," many managers overlook *transition costs,* the type of operating expense that kicks in when the organization switches from something old to something new. These costs might include a temporary spike in manufacturing defects, say, or an increase in calls to the help desk. Most major projects will cause some disruption, and you need to account for it in your estimates. The subject-matter experts on your team should be able to identify transition costs for their departments; these should be included as a separate line on our ROI worksheet.

Benefits

Benefits consist mainly of *revenue* (money you'll bring in through sales) and *productivity savings* (costs you'll avoid through greater efficiency). Let's look at each.

Revenue

Ask your sales and marketing subject-matter experts to work with you to estimate revenue. They'll help you set realistic targets—both how much to expect and when to expect it.

They'll also help you anticipate the response from competitors—a critical long-term factor. For example, the revenue stream for a new product may plateau or decrease when a rival comes to market with a similar or better offering. Look with your team at what's happened with previous products—and base your assumptions on that. Did sales grow steadily for the first three years and then decay once competitors entered the market?

When considering revenue, factor in the *cost of goods sold* (listed as COGS on the income statement). This puts a price tag on the materials and labor required to produce what you're selling. Of course, to do that, you'll first have to estimate how many units you'll sell each year—once again, your team members from sales and marketing can help with those numbers. People often neglect to take COGS into account and so accidentally inflate their revenue estimates. But your stakeholders will want to see that you've deducted them from your revenues—that's how you calculate your gross profit margin.

Productivity savings

Some productivity savings relate to product costs, others to overhead costs. You can achieve the former by changing materials or automating assembly. These savings change the product cost baseline and, therefore, the gross profit margin. You'll base these estimates on how many units you'll produce each year. By contrast, overhead productivity savings come from cutting current, ongoing expenses that stem from how you run the business. Maybe a security system you're proposing would enable your company to hire fewer guards without compromising safety. Such savings are usually flat—in other words, they are the same every year.

If you say your project will save personnel overhead costs, your stakeholders will probably ask, "Who are we going to lay off?"—and for good reason. Unless you get rid of people, you still have to pay them. Even if you make the argument that they'll do other things instead, you're not really saving money. You're just moving expenses around to other parts of the organization. But you might be able to cut other types of operating expenses: Maybe your initiative will eliminate the need for overtime or reduce costly errors by giving people more time to focus on their tasks. Or perhaps the company will spend less on maintenance contracts.

Intangible costs and benefits

Some costs and benefits are tough to measure. For example, a new employee time-tracking system may hurt morale—but how do you quantify the cost to the company? If a new product feature will increase overall customer satisfaction, how do you translate that benefit into dollars?

Whenever possible, assign numbers to your costs and benefits. Derive those figures from expected changes in behavior—those are the business consequences you can measure. If morale will be hurt, will you see an increase in absenteeism? By how much? What about error rates and training costs? How much will they go up? If customers will be happier, how many repeat customers will you gain? How much will you save in advertising as a result? If you think your new performance management system will improve employee satisfaction, how much will the turnover rate drop? And how much will that save the company in new-hire training?

If you truly can't quantify certain costs or benefits, you can't use them in your calculations—though you should still mention them when you present your case.

Where to Get the Numbers

As you've probably gathered by now, you're not making up these estimates alone in your office. You're reaching out to beneficiaries and experts in various departments to get accurate information. If you're proposing an initiative to improve the contracting process with vendors, get input from procurement. If your case is for a new product in a new market, ask sales and marketing colleagues how much revenue growth they expect and whether the product will cannibalize other offerings. The experts on your team have already helped you identify types of costs and benefits—now they can suggest actual numbers from their functions' perspectives.

Since it's nobody's job to give you the numbers you need, you have to rely on relationships—often going beyond your core team—to get them. If you're an IT manager proposing a new system to track sales leads, ask one of your contacts in sales to vet your costs and benefits. Don't have anyone to call? See if your manager or a member of your team can put you in touch with somebody.

When you're making a case for an entirely new type of project for your company, tap your broader professional network for figures, as you did when you were weighing various options and narrowing them down. Ask people in other companies what they've spent on similar projects. They're not going to hand over their detailed plans—those would be considered proprietary. But they may be willing to give you a ballpark number, saying that it cost them about $20 million to put in SAP software. You can also get general estimates from vendors, based on their experience doing similar work for other clients. If you work for a large corporation, ask other operating divisions for their input.

Whatever the source, don't take the numbers at face value. Your sales contact may give you five-year forecasts that seem low. Find out what he's basing them on, how they compare with other product sales, and whether he's willing to back up the numbers when you share them with the review committee. And keep in mind that certain departments are inclined to either pad or lowball numbers. Salespeople rewarded with commissions may underestimate so they can exceed their targets. Marketing colleagues, wanting to see a new product get approved, may give you a higher number. Understanding biases like these will help you ask the right questions to get the most accurate, balanced numbers possible. Of course, people won't tell you that their numbers are biased. They'll say that they're realistic. To assess how accurate their estimates are, ask them what the impact would be if the number were 20% higher or 20% lower. If you get an emotional response to such questions, there's a good chance that, whether they realize it or not, they've given you a biased number. In that case, check with another subject-matter expert to confirm the initial figures you received. If you've got a large range for one of your estimates, that signals a project risk. Select the value that you believe is most realistic and test the best-case and worst-case numbers (see chapter 11, "Account for Risks").

Only use—and present—numbers that have buy-in from the departments affected. When the CFO questions your forecasts, you want to be able to tell him that his team has endorsed them. If you can't back up numbers when stakeholders scrutinize them, your entire case loses credibility.

Again, this is where friends in the finance department can be enormously helpful in putting together estimates. They have insight into where money is spent across functions and quick access to those numbers. They're familiar with each line of the P&L, and they know what past projects have cost the company. If you don't have a helpful contact in finance already, it's worth your time to find one and cultivate that relationship. Ask your boss who supports your department in the finance group. Then reach out to the person and say you're interested in understanding your department's numbers and how your work can affect them. It's smart to do this right after the quarterly report comes out. Showing that interest will win you a friend, and you'll probably learn something along the way.

Track Where Each Number Comes From

As you gather figures, collect them in a spreadsheet like the one in chapter 10, "Calculate ROI" (see figure 10-1). You can tailor this spreadsheet to fit your circumstances. For instance, if you are doing an IT project, you'll forecast only three to five years out, not 10. List your costs and benefits—and capture the assumptions and sources along with them. This is critical information to have when it's time to do your risk analysis and present to stakeholders. For example, if one of your expenses is new software, list the amount, how many licenses it includes, and any other assumptions you've made about the price. Then document who gave you the estimate. Later, when you're asked where the number came from, you'll have the information right there in the spreadsheet.

Your completed spreadsheet may have 50 rows, or more than 100—whatever it takes to accurately cost out the project and account for its benefits. Tracking the source of your figures may sound tedious, but will save you time later. And being able to answer questions from the review committee during your presentation will definitely enhance your credibility.

Manage Uncertainty

You're dealing with estimates and forecasts, so work with round numbers. If you're forecasting sales, it's OK to say that you'll see $5 million the first year, $8 million the next year, and $12 million the year after that. No one expects you to have a detailed, 100% accurate list of costs and benefits at this point in the process.

In fact, many of your numbers will be educated guesses. I worked with a company a couple of years ago that wanted to install an ERP system. The IT manager building the case reached out to three of his contacts at other companies to ask what they had spent on similar systems. He got three wildly different numbers. Which did he use? The one in the middle. But he also ran the calculation using the high figure (considering it the worst case) and the low one (the best case). That's what you should do if there's a high level of uncertainty with some of your numbers. Identify a range, and use the middle number.

You can also reduce uncertainty by benchmarking your project against others your company has undertaken. These comparisons will often give you the most-accurate numbers because you're dealing with known systems, processes, and people.

Even so, some uncertainty will remain, and senior managers understand that. If you're off—say you initially estimate $7 million in costs but discover later that the project will run closer to $8 million—people probably won't blame you, demanding to know why you were wrong. More likely (assuming you've developed and presented a solid case), they'll ask, "OK, so what will $7 million get us?"

Ignore Sunk Costs

On occasion, you may do a business case for a project that's already in progress so stakeholders can decide whether to continue it or alter its direction. In a situation like that, you need to keep track of *sunk costs*—the money already spent—but don't include them in your estimates or ROI calculation. Know the total amount in case stakeholders have questions, but don't allow it to factor too heavily in their decision. If you do, they may choose to keep funding the project since they've already spent so much on it—and that's how companies dig themselves into gigantic financial holes.

Take an equipment rental company I worked with that wanted to go completely paperless. The project lead estimated that it would take three years and $25 million. Three years later, the company had spent $35 million, with only one quarter of the work done. The team redid the business case, wisely ignoring the $35 million already spent, and the stakeholders decided not to move forward—it wasn't worthwhile in light of all the hassles they now knew to expect.

Using the costs and benefits you've outlined, you can now calculate the return on your investment.

Chapter 10
Calculate ROI

Return on investment (ROI) is a more pointed look at the financial value of your proposal. Think of it as a measure of relative "goodness" because it helps organizations compare projects and decide which ones to pursue.

Good news for mathphobes: It takes nanoseconds to calculate ROI in a spreadsheet (Excel saves you from doing fifth-order partial differential equations by hand). Many companies have templates, like the one in figure 10-1, where you just plug in your numbers and the software does the rest.

Here's the classic formula for ROI:

ROI = Net Benefit/Total Cost
(Net benefit is the total benefit minus the total cost.)

A positive ROI is good. A negative one means the project's not worth doing. The larger the ROI value, the better the project. But this is a static measure that doesn't take into consideration changes to benefits and costs over time. Therefore, most companies use one of the more advanced, dynamic techniques described in figure 10-2.

FIGURE 10-1

Your basic ROI spreadsheet

Before selecting a method for calculating ROI, enter your costs and benefits into a spreadsheet like the one shown here. This serves as your starting point for any ROI technique.

Project estimating & approval   Worksheet

Project investment

	Amount	Year 1	Year 2	Year 3	Year 4	Year 5	Year 6	Year 7	Year 8	Year 9	Year 10	Estimate rationale
Capital												
Category 1 (ex: HW procurement)												
Category 2 (ex: Facility upgrade)												
Total capital costs	$ -											
Project expense (one-time expense)												
Category 1 (ex: Project personnel costs)												
Category 2 (ex: Project travel)												
Total project expense	$ -											
Total project investment	$ -	$ -	$ -	$ -	$ -	$ -	$ -	$ -	$ -	$ -	$ -	

Operating costs (OpEx)

	Amount	Year 1	Year 2	Year 3	Year 4	Year 5	Year 6	Year 7	Year 8	Year 9	Year 10	Estimate rationale
Category 1 (ex: SW license)												
Category 2 (ex: Maintenance)												
Total operating costs	$ -	$ -	$ -	$ -	$ -	$ -	$ -	$ -	$ -	$ -	$ -	

Project benefits (amount & timing)

	Amount	Year 1	Year 2	Year 3	Year 4	Year 5	Year 6	Year 7	Year 8	Year 9	Year 10	Estimate rationale
Sales benefits												
Incremental sales												
Infrastructure changes (savings +, costs -)												
Support personnel, etc. (list all)												
Operations impacts (savings +, costs -)												
Product support cost reduction												
Other benefits												
Total benefits		$ -	$ -	$ -	$ -	$ -	$ -	$ -	$ -	$ -	$ -	
Annual total	$	$ -	$ -	$ -	$ -	$ -	$ -	$ -	$ -	$ -	$ -	
Cumulative total	$	$ -	$ -	$ -	$ -	$ -	$ -	$ -	$ -	$ -	$ -	

FIGURE 10-2

Four ways to calculate ROI

Method	Answers the question...	Expressed in...	Typically used for...
Break-even analysis	How many sales do we need to recoup the investment?	Units sold	Market-focused projects, such as product development; entrepreneurial endeavors
Payback period	How long will it take to recoup the investment?	Months or years	Projects with a heavy up-front investment, such as facilities projects; productivity projects that accumulate benefits over time
Net present value	How much is this project worth to the business?	Dollars	Projects with large expenditures
Internal rate of return	What rate of return will this project deliver over its life cycle?	Percentage	Projects that the company reports on externally, especially those that require you to borrow money

The best method for you—break-even analysis, pay-back period, net present value (NPV), or internal rate of return (IRR)—will depend on the nature of your project and what's most important to the business. If your company has a standard approach, go with that so your stake-holders can easily compare your project with others. Or you may need to apply several methods to accommodate a variety of preferences.

Fortunately, you can start with the same basic spread-sheet shown in figure 10-1, no matter which techniques you use. Once you've loaded your estimates into that, you create other worksheets from it, with slight variations to perform the different types of calculations.

Break-Even Analysis

Break-even analysis tells you how many units you need to sell in order to pay for the project (see figure 10-3). Companies typically use it for new products and other projects that have a marketing focus—they weigh their analysis against the size of the market opportunity. This technique doesn't reveal how *long* it takes to break even, so it's most useful when you're unsure about timing—when the project will start, how long it will last, and so on. Entrepreneurs often use break-even analysis to show investors how many units must be sold before they'll turn a profit.

It's not the best method when you have high, time-dependent operating costs or infrastructure benefits that aren't related to product volume, since it's impossible to quantify the impact of those factors on unit sales. In those cases, you'll probably want to determine NPV instead.

FIGURE 10-3

Break-even example

When you tailor your basic ROI worksheet to determine your break-even point, it should look like this.

Project estimating & approval

Break-even

Project investment

Capital	Amount	Estimate rationale
Category 1 *(ex: HW procurement)*	$ -	none
Total capital costs	$ -	
Project expense (one-time expense)		
Concept analysis	$ (50,000)	similar to project XYZ
Development	$ (300,000)	similar to project XYZ
Test and validation	$ (100,000)	based on current compliance matrix
Industrialization and commercialization	$ (50,000)	similar to project XYZ
Total project expense	$ (500,000)	
Total project investment	**$ (500,000)**	

Operating costs (OpEx)

	Amount	
Category 1 *(ex: SW license)*	$ -	none
Total operating costs	$ -	

Project benefits (amount & timing)

	Amount	
Sales benefits		
Incremental sales	$300,000/Year	sales increase by $1M with $1K price and 30% gross margin rate per Bob in mktg
Infrastructure changes (savings +, costs -)		none
Operations impacts (savings +, costs -)		reduction in warranty and help desk costs per Sue in service
Product support cost reduction	$100,000/Year	
Other benefits		none
Total benefits	$ -	

To calculate your break-even point, you'll first determine the gross profit margin from selling one unit of your product:

$$\text{Revenue} - \text{COGS} = \text{Gross Margin}$$

Then you can figure out how many units you need to sell for your sales benefit to equal your total costs:

$$\text{Break-Even Number of Units} = \text{Net Project Cost/Gross Margin}$$

Here's what those calculations look like when you plug in numbers from the spreadsheet in figure 10-3.

Our gross margin from selling one unit is $300. (See "Estimate Rationale" for sales benefits in the spreadsheet: 30% of $1,000 is $300. If you don't already know the gross margin, calculate it by subtracting COGS from revenue, as described above.) And in this case, we'll get our net project cost ($400,000) by adding one year of the productivity benefit ($100,000) to the total project investment ($-$500,000).

Now we can enter these numbers into our break-even formula:

$$\text{Break-Even Number of Units} = \$400,000/\$300$$

We'll break even when we sell 1,334 units (rounding up from 1,333.33 because we can't sell one-third of a unit).

Payback Period

Payback period, one of the simplest ways of calculating ROI that accounts for time, tells you how long it will take to earn back the money invested.

You can create a basic payback spreadsheet that lists the total costs and benefits and spreads them over time, either by month or year (usually the latter—see figures 10-4 and 10-5 for examples). You'll determine period totals by summing each month's or year's numbers—these reflect the monthly or annual cash flow. And then you'll figure out the cumulative cash flow by adding period totals.

Typically, you'll start off with a negative cash flow because you're spending on the project but you haven't yet reaped the benefits. Eventually, benefits should offset costs. The payback point occurs when the cumulative cash flow changes from negative to positive—that's when the cumulative benefits exceed the cumulative costs.

You can start your timing for payback either after you complete the project, when benefits kick in (as in figure 10-4, which shows what's known as Type 0), or when the project work begins, to capture the time and money invested throughout (as in figure 10-5, which shows Type 1). Neither approach is better or worse. Just make sure you're following your company's standard or you agree with stakeholders ahead of time on which method to use.

In our Type 0 example (figure 10-4), when the project is done, we start off $500,000 in the hole. Then, in Year 1, we gain $400,000 in benefit—so we're still $100,000 in the negative, but we're making our way out. The project goes positive in Year 2, so we know the payback period will be one full year plus some fraction of the second year. To figure that out, take the last year of negative cumulative cash flow (Year 1) and using the absolute value of that

FIGURE 10-4

Type 0 payback example

To calculate payback starting from project completion, use a Type 0 spreadsheet. The first column (labeled "Project") captures costs incurred throughout the project, whether it takes a few months or a few years to complete. Benefits appear in the second column (Year 1) and subsequent columns.

Project estimating & approval — Type 0 payback

Project investment

	Amount	Project	Year 1	Year 2	Year 3	Estimate rationale
Capital	$ -					none
Category 1 (ex: HW procurement)	$ -					
Total capital costs						
Project expense (one-time expense)						
Concept analysis	$ (50,000)	$ (50,000)				similar to project XYZ
Development	$ (300,000)	$ (300,000)				similar to project XYZ
Test and validation	$ (100,000)	$ (100,000)				based on current compliance matrix
Industrialization and commercialization	$ (50,000)	$ (50,000)				similar to project XYZ
Total project expense	$ (500,000)	$ (500,000)				
Total project investment	**$ (500,000)**	**$ (500,000)**	**$ -**	**$ -**	**$ -**	

Operating costs (OpEx)	Amount	Project	Year 1	Year 2	Year 3	
Category 1 (ex: SW license)	$ -	$ -	$ -	$ -	$ -	none
Total operating costs		$ -	$ -	$ -	$ -	

Project benefits (amount & timing)	Amount	Project	Year 1	Year 2	Year 3	
Sales benefits						sales increase by $1M with $1K price and 30% gross margin rate per Bob in mktg
Incremental sales	$300,000/Year		$ 300,000	$ 300,000	$ 300,000	
Infrastructure changes (savings +, costs -)						none
Operations impacts (savings +, costs -)						reduction in warranty and help desk costs per
Product cost savings	$100,000/Year		$ 100,000	$ 100,000	$ 100,000	Sue in service
Other benefits	$ -					none
Total benefits		$ -	$ 400,000	$ 400,000	$ 400,000	

	Project	Year 1	Year 2	Year 3
Annual total	$ (500,000)	$ 400,000	$ 400,000	$ 400,000
Cumulative total	$ (500,000)	$ (100,000)	$ 300,000	$ 700,000

FIGURE 10-5

Type 1 Payback Example

In a Type 1 spreadsheet, you begin calculating the payback period from the day you launch the project. Each column typically represents one year. If the project takes less than a year to complete, the first column will contain both project costs and benefits. If it takes more than a year, the first column will have only project costs; benefits will appear in a later column.

Project estimating & approval — Type 1 payback

Project investment

	Amount	Year 1	Year 2	Year 3	Year 4	Estimate rationale
Capital						
Category 1 (ex: HW procurement)	$ -					none
Total capital costs	$ -					
Project expense (one-time expense)						
Concept analysis	$ (50,000)	$ (50,000)				similar to project XYZ
Development	$ (300,000)	$ (300,000)				similar to project XYZ
Test and validation	$ (100,000)	$ (50,000)	$ (50,000)			based on current compliance matrix
Industrialization and commercialization	$ (50,000)		$ (50,000)			similar to project XYZ
Total project expense	$ (500,000)					
Total project investment	$ (500,000)	$ (400,000)	$ (100,000)	$ -	$ -	

Operating costs (OpEx)

	Amount	Year 1	Year 2	Year 3	Year 4	
Category 1 (ex: SW license)	$ -					none
Total operating costs		$ -	$ -	$ -	$ -	

Project benefits (amount & timing)

	Amount	Year 1	Year 2	Year 3	Year 4	Estimate rationale
Sales benefits						
Incremental sales	$300,000/Year		$ 225,000	$ 300,000	$ 300,000	sales increase by $1M with $1k price and 30% gross margin rate per Bob in mktg
Infrastructure changes (savings +, costs -)						none
Operations impacts (savings +, costs -)						reduction in warranty and help desk costs per Sue in service
Product cost savings	$100,000/Year		$ 75,000	$ 100,000	$ 100,000	
Other benefits	$ -					none
Total benefits	$ -	$ 300,000	$ 400,000	$ 400,000		

	Year 1	Year 2	Year 3	Year 4
Annual total	$ (400,000)	$ 200,000	$ 400,000	$ 400,000
Cumulative total	$ (400,000)	$ (200,000)	$ 200,000	$ 600,000

year's cumulative total, divide by the following year's annual cash flow.

In this case, it's $100,000 divided by $400,000, or .25 (note that we drop the negative of the first figure—we're using the absolute value). It will take us 1.25 years to recoup our investment.

Now take a look at our Type 1 example (figure 10–5). By the end of Year 1, we'll have racked up most of our project costs ($400,000), with no benefits to show for them yet. In Year 2, we'll spend another $100,000 in the first three months to finish the project, but that's offset by productivity savings and new sales in the final nine months, so we'll be $200,000 in the hole at year-end. In Year 3, we'll get the full $400,000 of benefit.

To figure out our payback period in Type 1, we take the last year that our cumulative cash flow was still negative (Year 2) and again using the absolute value of that year's cumulative cash flow, divide by the following year's annual cash flow (in this case, $200,000 divided by $400,000). So it will be 2.5 years before we recoup our investment.

With each type of calculation, you get completely different numbers. Companies often use Type 0 to analyze smaller projects with uncertain time frames. For larger projects that tie up a lot of money, companies prefer Type 1 because they want to know when they're going to get the investment back. But to use Type 1, you need to have a good sense of how long the project will take—otherwise, your calculations will be way off.

One downside of the payback period method: It doesn't show what happens after you earn the money back. Let's say you'll recoup the investment in a new product in two years, and after that you expect exponential sales growth. With this technique, your stakeholders wouldn't know the difference between your product and a similar one for which sales start to decay after two years. If your company uses the payback calculation as its standard but you expect benefits to increase or decrease significantly after the payback point, you should calculate net present value as well.

Net Present Value (NPV)

Net present value (NPV) shows today's value of a long-term investment by discounting future cash flows, so you can see what the impact of your 10-year project would be in today's dollars. This is my preferred method for calculating ROI—I believe it gives the most complete view of a project's value. Both NPV and the next technique, IRR, rely on the principle of the time value of money, which states that the buying power of money today is greater than the buying power of the same amount of money in the future.

If the NPV is negative, the project is not a good one. It will ultimately drain cash from the business, and you shouldn't even bring it to the table. If it's positive, you can make a solid case for the project. The larger the positive number, the greater the benefit.

NPV is particularly useful in comparing the intrinsic value of two mutually exclusive projects. Your stakeholders can look at the NPV of your project and a completely different one and make a fair comparison.

Here's the calculation:

$$\text{Net Present Value} = \sum \frac{\text{Year n Total Cash Flow}}{(1 + \text{Discount Rate})^n}$$

Where "n" is the year whose cash flow is being discounted.

This is the sum of the present value of cash flows (positive and negative) for each year associated with the investment, discounted so that it's expressed in today's dollars.

Luckily, you don't have to do this by hand. Excel does it for you when you enter the stream of costs and benefits over a set time period.

As you can see, the example in figure 10-6 has a high NPV compared with the level of investment (even $1 in the positive is considered good). We'd have a strong chance of getting that project approved, as long as it's aligned with business objectives and not up against projects with a higher value.

Assuming your project costs will only be accurate to plus or minus 25%, don't recommend an option with an NPV that's less than 25% of the project cost. Otherwise, stakeholders might worry that once the project gets started, the true NPV will be closer to $0.

One note about the formula: The "NPV" function in Excel starts discounting the first year inside the formula. However, any costs or benefits in the current year shouldn't be discounted—they're already in today's dollars. So you'll need to remove the value for the current year from the Excel NPV formula and manually add that to your total NPV for the remaining years.

FIGURE 10-6

NPV example

Calculate NPV when you want to show the value of a long-term investment in today's dollars.

Project estimating & approval   NPV

Project investment

Capital	Amount	Year 1	Year 2	Year 3	Year 4	Year 5	Year 6	Estimate rationale
Category 1 (ex: HW procurement)	$ -							
Total capital costs	$ -							none
Project expense (one-time expense)								
Concept analysis	$ (50,000)	$ (50,000)						similar to project XYZ
Development	$ (300,000)	$ (300,000)						similar to project XYZ
Test and validation	$ (100,000)	$ (50,000)	$ (50,000)					based on current compliance matrix
Industrialization and commercialization	$ (50,000)		$ (50,000)					similar to project XYZ
Total project expense	$ (500,000)							
Total project investment	**$ (500,000)**	**$ (400,000)**	**$ (100,000)**	**$ -**	**$ -**	**$ -**	**-**	

Operating costs (OpEx)

	Amount	Year 1	Year 2	Year 3	Year 4	Year 5	Year 6	
Category 1 (ex: SW license)	$ -							
Total operating costs		**$ -**	**$ -**	**$ -**	**$ -**	**$ -**	**-**	none

Project benefits (amount & timing)

	Amount	Year 1	Year 2	Year 3	Year 4	Year 5	Year 6	
Sales benefits								
Incremental sales	$300,000/Year		$ 225,000	$ 300,000	$ 300,000	$ 300,000	$ 300,000	sales increase by $1M with $1K price and 30% gross margin rate per Bob in mktg
Infrastructure changes (savings +, costs -)								none
Operations impacts (savings +, costs -)								
Product support cost reduction	$100,000/Year		$ 75,000	$ 100,000	$ 100,000	$ 100,000	$ 100,000	reduction in warranty and help desk costs per Sue in service
Other benefits	$ -							none
Total benefits			**$ 300,000**	**$ 400,000**	**$ 400,000**	**$ 400,000**	**$ 400,000**	

		Year 1	Year 2	Year 3	Year 4	Year 5	Year 6
	Annual total	$ (400,000)	$ 200,000	$ 400,000	$ 400,000	$ 400,000	$ 400,000

NPV: $1,011,899

Discount rate: 8.0%

CHOOSING A DISCOUNT RATE FOR NPV

To calculate NPV, you need to include a discount rate in your formula. This is tied to the current cost of money. It will change from year to year, depending on the health of the company, the health of the economy, and your stakeholders' risk tolerance. In today's economy, most companies are using 5% to 10%. In a good economy, they'll use 10% to 15%. Someone in finance can probably tell you what rate to use, or it will already be filled in on your company's template. If this isn't the case, or if you're an entrepreneur, you can use your company's interest rate or the prime rate (whichever is higher) plus 5%.

Internal Rate of Return (IRR)

Internal rate of return (IRR) shows a project's investment value. It essentially tells you what rate of return you would get if you invested the same amount of money in a CD that performed as well as your project.

If the IRR is small, you shouldn't do the project—there are better ways to spend your money. If it's large, you have a good shot at approval (as with NPV, the greater the rate, the greater the benefit). Finance experts often use this technique to determine whether it's worth borrowing money for a project. Bankers will want to know the return rate on the money they lend, to make sure your company can pay back the interest and principal.

Entrepreneurs, take note: Investors often want to understand the IRR in the same way that bankers do. The rate of return indicates what they can expect to receive from their investment when they cash out.

Here's the calculation:

$$0 = \sum \frac{\text{Year n Total Cash Flow}}{(1 + \text{Rate of Return})^n}$$

Where "n" is the year whose cash flow is being discounted.

Again, thank goodness for software.

Many people run IRR when they run NPV since both use the same numbers, and it's just another formula in the spreadsheet. The example in figure 10-7 shows an IRR of 72.4%—a great result. You're not likely to get that much of a return on other types of investments.

What to Do with Negative or Low Numbers

When your calculations show a negative NPV or a very low IRR, for example, you need to reevaluate the case you're trying to make. If the project was your idea, go back and check your assumptions and numbers carefully. Unless you find errors, it may be time to pull the plug on your case. Stakeholders usually won't approve a project that doesn't return value to the company (occasional exceptions apply—more on this later).

By contrast, if you were assigned the business case, your beneficiaries may insist that the project is necessary even if the numbers don't support it. In a situation like that, go ahead and present the case with the bad ROI—but provide stakeholders with other viable options. Suppose your sales team decides that the company needs a certain new product to compete in the low-price market, and you're tapped to develop the case. After running the

FIGURE 10-7

IRR example

You calculate IRR to determine your project's investment value. It's a useful metric if you want to borrow funds from a bank, for example, or attract investors for a start-up venture.

Project estimating & approval   IRR

Project investment	Amount	Year 1	Year 2	Year 3	Year 4	Year 5	Year 6	Estimate rationale
Capital								
Category 1 (ex: HW procurement)	$ -							none
Total capital costs	$ -							
Project expense (one-time expense)								
Concept analysis	$ (50,000)	$ (50,000)						similar to project XYZ
Development	$ (300,000)	$ (300,000)						similar to project XYZ
Test and validation	$ (100,000)	$ (50,000)	$ (50,000)					based on current compliance matrix
Industrialization and commercialization	$ (50,000)		$ (50,000)					similar to project XYZ
Total project expense	$ (500,000)							
Total project investment	$ (500,000)	$ (400,000)	$ (100,000)	$ -	$ -	$ -	-	

Operating costs (OpEx)	Amount	Year 1	Year 2	Year 3	Year 4	Year 5	Year 6	
Category 1 (ex: SW license)	$ -	$ -	$ -	$ -	$ -	$ -	-	none
Total operating costs		$ -	$ -	$ -	$ -	$ -	-	

Project benefits (amount & timing)	Amount	Year 1	Year 2	Year 3	Year 4	Year 5	Year 6	
Sales benefits								
Incremental sales	$300,000/Year		$ 225,000	$ 300,000	$ 300,000	$ 300,000	$ 300,000	sales increase by $1M with $1K price and 30% gross margin rate per Bob in mktg
Infrastructure changes (savings +, costs -)								none
Operations impacts (savings +, costs -)	$100,000/Year		$ 75,000	$ 100,000	$ 100,000	$ 100,000	$ 100,000	reduction in warranty and help desk costs per Sue in service
Product support cost reduction	$ -							none
Other benefits	$ -							none
Total benefits		$ -	$ 300,000	$ 400,000	$ 400,000	$ 400,000	$ 400,000	

Annual total $ (400,000) $ 200,000 $ 400,000 $ 400,000 $ 400,000 $ 400,000

IRR: 72.4%

numbers, you get a negative NPV. Perhaps the competitor has patent protection or a strong hold on the market that you don't think you can crack. Present the case, but also suggest another way to address the sales team's concerns. Maybe your company should take out features to bring down the product's price, for instance, or go to that market with a different type of offering.

In some cases, such as compliance projects, you can expect a negative return because you'll get no new revenue or productivity (although staying in business is obviously a benefit). Say you have to meet new air-emissions standards or upgrade your financial reporting system to comply with a new regulation. The numbers won't be good, but you may have to do the project anyway. The medical device folks I worked with needed to get rid of certain product materials that the FDA had deemed potentially hazardous. They'd been making products with some of these materials for 20 years, so they had to go through major redesigns. They're now in the process of removing more than 20 materials that are no longer compliant—a major investment that doesn't show any increase in sales or productivity. But they have to do it to sell compliant products.

When evaluating projects, stakeholders look for the best numbers: the lowest break-even point, the quickest payback period, or the highest NPV or IRR. But that's not all they base their decision on. Remember that you are telling a story to convince them your project is worthwhile—the ROI number is just one data point.

Chapter 11
Account for Risks

After you've run the ROI, you still have some number crunching left to do. None of the ROI techniques will account for risks, so it's a separate step to identify them and consider what impact they'll have on your final figures.

Gut-Check the Numbers

If you're looking at a low ROI and thinking, "Wait—I thought this was going to be a great project," question your numbers. Could you have underestimated revenue? Or overestimated transition costs? Or entered a wrong figure? (As you'd imagine, leaving off a zero makes a big difference.) Scrutinize each line item and ask whether the number—or the timing—could be off.

You may need to go back to your subject-matter experts and ask them to double-check their estimates. For example: "Can we get 20% more in sales? What would you need to deliver that?" Or: "Can we train call center employees on the new system sooner?"

You've based every line of your spreadsheet on assumptions—which you've carefully documented. But what if they're wrong and things don't go as you planned? What if the worst (or best) case occurs?

Analyzing risk helps you see what will happen to the project's value if your assumptions are off. Most people focus on threats. (What if the vendor doesn't deliver on time? What if the cost of raw materials goes through the roof?) But you need to consider opportunities as well. (How can you get a higher NPV or a faster payback? Can you complete the project sooner? Can you put your best team on it?) Go through your estimates line by line and consider what factors might alter them. For instance:

- **Personnel:** What if the person running this project leaves the company? What if you don't get all the resources you requested? Or conversely: What if you're able to pull together an all-star team or hire an outside expert?

- **Technology:** What if you encounter bugs when testing? What if employees struggle to adapt to the new system? What if you run into intellectual-property issues with the technology?

- **Quality/Performance:** What if the product doesn't perform as you expect it to—for better or worse? What if quality suffers because of a tight schedule?

- **Scope:** What if the project needs to include more (or fewer) geographic regions, employees, or customers? What if the stakeholders change requirements? What if a regulatory change creates a new opportunity?

- **Schedule:** What if you aren't able to hit the launch date? What would allow you to get ahead of schedule? Does anything outside the project need to happen before you can complete it?

Think about what concerns your stakeholders will have. Where will they see risks? Does your CTO always assume projects take twice as long as planned? Does your CMO distrust any project that relies on vendors? Identify the questions they might ask so you can account for them in your calculations and, ultimately, in your presentation. Once you've listed the risks, identify your biggest threats and opportunities (see figure 11-1): Which are most likely to happen, and which would have the greatest impact on

FIGURE 11-1

Assessing threats and opportunities

When reviewing project risks with decision makers, draw their attention to the threats and opportunities with the highest probability and impact—those that would fall in the upper-right corner of this matrix.

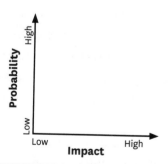

your project? Those are the ones to highlight when you present to your stakeholders.

Test the Numbers

In light of the risks you've identified, rerun your calculations. What happens if your project costs run over by 20%? How does that change the NPV? What if the product launches six months later than you expected (see figure 11-2)?

Play with the numbers. Plug in your best guess for each line, then the best- and worst-case figures, and see what happens to your spreadsheets. You're likely to choose a middle number for most lines, but you may have reason to be conservative or aggressive on certain items. If one of your critical stakeholders is risk-averse, for example, you may go with lower numbers on your benefit stream. If you face severe penalties for completing the project late, you may want to build some buffer into your timing assumptions. Conservative assumptions lower your risk; aggressive assumptions increase it. Often you can mention contingencies and say that the team will develop plans for them when it's time to put together a detailed project plan—but sometimes stakeholders want to know up front what types of contingencies you're considering.

Ultimately, each number you settle on is a judgment call. Check with your subject-matter experts, your manager, and your project champion for feedback on major costs and benefits. Do your final figures seem reasonable to them?

As you tinker, you'll start to see what it would take to get the best ROI figure. But you need to present realistic

FIGURE 11-2

Factoring risks into your spreadsheets

When calculating ROI, you'll consider many "what ifs" and adjust your numbers to reflect likely scenarios. In this example, which uses estimates from Figure 10-6, a six-month project delay stretches the project costs, delays the benefit start, and causes a 26% drop in NPV (see shaded cells).

Project estimating & approval   NPV with six-month project delay

Project investment

Capital	Amount	Year 1	Year 2	Year 3	Year 4	Year 5	Year 6	Estimate rationale
Category 1 (ex: HW procurement)	$ -							none
Total capital costs	$ -							
Project expense (one-time expense)								
Concept analysis	$ (50,000)	$ (50,000)						similar to project RST
Development	$ (300,000)	$ (200,000)	$ (100,000)					similar to project RST
Test and validation	$ (100,000)		$ (100,000)					based on current compliance matrix
Industrialization and commercialization	$ (50,000)		$ (50,000)					similar to project RST
Total project expense	$ (500,000)							
Total project investment	**$ (500,000)**	**$ (250,000)**	**$ (250,000)**	**$ -**	**$ -**	**$ -**	**$ -**	

Operating costs (OpEx)

	Amount	Year 1	Year 2	Year 3	Year 4	Year 5	Year 6	
Category 1 (ex: SW License)	$ -							none
Total operating costs		**$ -**	**$ -**	**$ -**	**$ -**	**$ -**	**$ -**	

Project benefits (amount & timing)

	Amount	Year 1	Year 2	Year 3	Year 4	Year 5	Year 6	
Sales benefits								
Incremental sales	$300,000/Year			$ 300,000	$ 300,000	$ 300,000	$ 300,000	sales increase by $1M with $1K price and 30% gross margin rate per Bob in mktg
Infrastructure changes (savings +, costs -)								none
Operations impacts (savings +, costs -)								reduction in warranty and help desk costs per Sue in service
Product support cost reduction	$100,000/Year			$ 100,000	$ 100,000	$ 100,000	$ 100,000	
Other benefits	$ -							none
Total benefits		**$ -**	**$ -**	**$ 400,000**	**$ 400,000**	**$ 400,000**	**$ 400,000**	

	Annual total	$ (250,000)	$ (250,000)	$ 400,000	$ 400,000	$ 400,000	$ 400,000	
	NPV:	**$745,232**						

Discount rate:	8.0%

risks, not just ones that make the case look good. Change an assumption if you have reason to believe it is wrong. Use wisdom and experience to make these decisions— don't pick arbitrary numbers to pad or manipulate your ROI. And make your risk assessment consistent with the numbers you have selected.

All of your information gathering, pressure-testing, and documenting sources will pay off as you assemble your winning presentation.

Section 5
Present Your Case and Move Forward

Chapter 12
Prepare Your Document

To get buy-in from your stakeholders, you must tell your "story" in a compelling way so they'll easily grasp the need, the solution (or solutions) you're proposing, and the benefits to the company. Typically, your audience will care most about ROI and how your project relates to strategic objectives—so keep those issues front and center. (See appendix B: How to Give a Killer Presentation by TED curator Chris Anderson for further advice on crafting your story, finding the right mix of data and narrative, and sharpening your delivery.) Here are some things to keep in mind as you prepare your presentation.

Your Document Should Speak for Itself

In some companies, especially large ones, you may not get to present your case. You might simply submit a Word document, Excel file, or slide deck and wait for the committee's decision. Or you might have just a few minutes in front of stakeholders who are considering 40 projects in a half-day meeting. Increasingly, companies decide on projects over conference calls or videoconferences to include stakeholders in different locations—so you can't even assume that your audience will pay undivided attention to your pitch. People may multitask, catching up on e-mail or getting other work done during the call.

For all those reasons, your document needs to stand on its own. Stakeholders must be able to comprehend the case without your voice-over. So don't distribute a deck as thick as a dictionary. Keep your slides crisp, clear, and to the point. But share enough data to show that you've done your homework.

Follow your company's process for presenting cases. Some firms want you to fill out forms or templates. That helps them review a large number of projects in one batch and make fair comparisons. Sure, the process may feel bureaucratic, but if you want your case approved, you have to go through the system.

Look at Past Presentations

Whether or not there's a standard format, find out what other presenters in your company have done. This will give you ideas for your own presentation—and a sense of what stakeholders might expect from you. Reach out to several coworkers who have recently gotten approval for business cases and ask to see their documents. Look for similarities. Did your colleagues use PowerPoint or Word? How did they describe the business need? What kind of data did they include in backup slides? How did they render the data? Also get your hands on a few rejected cases, if you can, to see what their project leads did differently. Did they fail to address risk? Were their documents too long or not substantial enough?

Make a Structured Argument

If your company doesn't provide templates and you can't track down helpful examples, you may need to start from scratch. In that case, I recommend the following structure:

1. **Opening slide:** Begin with an executive summary that briefly states the problem or opportunity, describes how you plan to address it, and explains why your solution is sensible and its expected ROI.

2. **Business need:** Describe why you're proposing the project. Explicitly connect the need to the company's strategic goals, and share data points that convey its urgency.

3. **Project overview:** Give a high-level description of the solution. If it's a new product, lay out the general concept and explain how it fits with existing offerings. For a productivity initiative (such as an IT project), specify which business processes it will affect and which costs it will eliminate or reduce. For a facility project, describe its magnitude, and name the facility systems it will touch (power, HVAC, water, sewage, and so on).

TELLING YOUR STORY IN THE EXECUTIVE SUMMARY

Your stakeholders are extremely busy, with competing demands on their time and attention. So think of your executive summary as a hook: It's a concise, compelling story about the business need, your solution, and the impact your solution will have.

Here's an example:

Executive Summary

We're facing tough new competitors in our Southeast Asian market—and losing a lot of sales as a result [the need]. So I'm proposing a new product that will help us regain market share [the solution]. When we get it out through our distribution channels, we expect to see sales double within the first six weeks—and we'll recoup our investment in just under three years [the impact].

Of course, if you're presenting with slides, you'll want to break up the text, perhaps like this:

Executive Summary

Problem:

- *Tough new competitors in Southeast Asia*
- *Loss of market share*

Solution:

- *New product*

Benefits:

- *Double sales in first six weeks*
- *Recoup investment in fewer than three years*

Clearly state the result of your ROI calculation: Above, it's the payback period of *fewer than three years*. But use whatever figure your stakeholders care most about: *The NPV is $20,000*. Or: *We'll get $30 million in new sales*. Or: *We'll cut $1.5 million in costs*.

Display the ROI prominently—it's the satisfying ending to your story. Then, in the rest of your document or presentation, demonstrate with data and other supporting material why your audience should have confidence in that story.

4. **Schedule and team:** Provide a high-level project plan. Include basic milestones, major deliverables, and core team members (by name or function).

5. **Impact:** Describe the benefits. Say which departments the project will affect, and how. Quantify the impact as precisely as you can.

6. **Risk:** Explain what might not go as planned— whether positive or negative. Include major risks associated both with doing the project and with not doing it.

7. **Financials:** Summarize the costs and benefits, and restate the ROI.

8. **Closing slide:** Restate the need, why your solution is a good one, and, once again, the ROI.

How long you make each section and how much supporting material you include will depend on how much time you have to present and your stakeholders' appetite for data. Again, use other successful cases as guides.

Your opening slide is crucial. It grabs reviewers' attention and sets the stage for everything to come (see sidebar "Telling Your Story in the Executive Summary"). And remember, you may not get beyond the opening slide if your review committee is busy or distracted. In fact, one time when I presented a business case at GE, previous presenters had gone long, and members of the review committee needed to wrap things up—they had to catch a plane. So I got five minutes to make my case (I was scheduled for 30 minutes). I did the presentation using only my executive summary slide and told reviewers they could find details in the rest of the deck. My project was one of the few they approved that day.

Document in hand, it's time to gather more feedback before you go in front of the official review committee.

Chapter 13
Shop Your Case Around

You've drafted your case, but you're not ready to present it just yet. First, you need to get buy-in from your stakeholders—because you'll want allies in the room when tough questions come up.

Two people in particular are critical: the head of the department that will lead the work and the head of the department that will benefit most from it. With these individuals on board, you'll defuse many concerns and greatly increase your chances of getting that green light.

Work with Your Champion

Go back to the champion you identified early in the case-development process. Ideally, you've asked for her input and kept her updated all along. But if not, definitely connect before the presentation.

If your champion believes in the value of your project, she'll defend it against naysayers or play a critical role in a tie-breaker situation.

Meet with Other Stakeholders in Advance

It's also helpful to give individuals on the review committee a preview and ask about their concerns. Get feedback from as many stakeholders as you can—you want to know where they stand, especially on new projects that are out of the ordinary for your company.

If you can't schedule meetings with them, you might be able to reach out through your subject-matter experts. Enlist a team member who is close to someone on the review board to go over the highlights with her. He might mention that he helped develop the business case and thinks it's a good project. He can then share her reaction with you and relay any questions or concerns she had.

Most questions you'll get at this point shouldn't come as a surprise if you've thoroughly prepared your case. (You know the CMO will ask about brand implications of the new product feature. Or that the CFO doesn't want to approve any projects over $5 million this year.) But on occasion, you'll discover concerns that haven't come up yet. It's always better to bring them to the surface before review time. Big surprises during the review meeting may sink your case and will almost certainly delay a decision. Of course, you'll need to adjust your content in response to what you hear. You may drop some features, for example, or tweak a few numbers. Let your stakeholders know you've made changes to allay their concerns so they can give the project their support at the review meeting.

Anticipate New Concerns

Other issues may arise when the committee is in the room, comparing your case with others.

Anticipate those concerns by getting inside the heads of your stakeholders: What do they care most about? What are their hot buttons? Ask around to find out what happened in similar review meetings. What unexpected questions came up? What issues became sticking points?

And think carefully about what's been going on in the business over the past week or month. Recent events can play a big role in review meetings. At a pharmaceutical company I worked with, the focus one year was growth, so people knew to explain how their proposed projects would grow sales, increase market share, or expand the customer base. But two days before the review committee met, one of the company's products got recalled. Quality hadn't been a major concern a few days earlier—and now, suddenly, it was the top priority. Stakeholders grilled project leads on quality assurance, testing, validation, and clinical trial strategy. They rejected cases that weren't airtight on quality, no matter how much growth those projects promised.

Size Up the Competition

Find out what other business cases are being considered. Talk with your boss to see if he knows of any initiatives up for approval. Ask your subject-matter experts (particularly those in finance) if they've been consulted about other projects. You probably won't change your numbers or general approach to beat out another project, but you might change what you emphasize in your presentation. If six other projects focus on market differentiation, as yours does, you may want to play up other benefits as well to distinguish your case.

Now that you've had a chance to socialize your case and gather and incorporate feedback, you're almost ready to go before the board. Time to quickly double-check that you have everything you need to deliver a great presentation.

Chapter 14
Are You Ready to Present?

Congratulations—you've developed your business case, and now you're ready to present it. Or are you?

Use this checklist to confirm that you've covered all your bases. If you answer "no" to any of these questions, go back and rework your case.

Did You . . .

☐ Lay out a clear business need and frame it as a compelling story that will grab stakeholders' attention?

☐ Align your objectives with strategic priorities, directly connecting your case to one of the company's stated goals?

☐ Identify each stakeholder's objectives and address as many as possible?

☐ Meet with your beneficiaries and accurately capture their needs?

☐ Identify a champion on the review committee who will support your project in front of the group?

☐ Consult subject-matter experts in different departments or functions to estimate costs and benefits, assess risks, calculate ROI, and get buy-in?

☐ Factor in transition costs?

☐ Document the assumptions behind each estimate—and note the source of each number?

☐ Double-check the numbers?

☐ Consider best- and worst-case scenarios?

☐ Consider several viable solutions along with the one you're proposing?

☐ Meet with stakeholders to preview your case and ask for input?

☐ Gain support from the department that will do the work?

☐ Gain support from the department that will benefit most from the project?

☐ Create a clear, concise document or slide deck?

☐ Gather enough information to move immediately into project planning if you get the green light?

Chapter 15
Make Your Pitch

On decision day, some stakeholders focus entirely on ROI. Others want to know who you worked with to gather information. Still others scrutinize the risk plan. If one person will decide your project's fate, play to her preferences. But when presenting to multiple stakeholders, include something for everyone.

Start with the Need

If stakeholders don't believe you've identified a real business need that's connected to the company's strategic priorities, they'll stop listening—or even ask you to stop talking. So describe that need at the outset, and remember to tell it like a story to engage your audience.

Be Brief

Review each slide, providing only pertinent information on major points. Your busy stakeholders will appreciate a concise, direct presentation. And don't just read your slides to them—you'll bore them to tears. As communication expert Nancy Duarte suggests in the *HBR Guide to Persuasive Presentations,* you can use the "notes" field in PowerPoint to spell out everything you want to say without projecting teleprompter text on the wall for everyone to see.

While reviewing the proposed solution, you might explain other alternatives you considered and then ruled out. Or when talking about risks, you might share the perspective of an important team member. But touch on these things quickly, then move on. Stay away from tangents. Many managers make the mistake of going deep into the risks, trying to head off doubts. It's better to mention them at a high level. For instance: *We thought about product introduction, technology transfer, and supplier issues and have included ways to mitigate these issues.* Stakeholders will request more detail if they want it—and then you can speak directly to their concerns.

Personalize the Presentation

Involve your beneficiaries and stakeholders in the discussion. If you're talking about the need, turn to the stakeholder who's feeling the most pain and invite her to comment on it. You might say something like, "Because this product line hasn't lived up to expectations, sales won't make its numbers"—and then ask the sales VP for quick observations on what's happening in the field. You might also have finance chime in with how much gross profit the company is short. This will enroll people in building and supporting your case in front of their peers.

Shine a Light on Your Experts

In some instances, stakeholders will be more (or less) inclined to approve your project depending on which subject-matter experts you worked with. You've chosen your team members carefully for their smarts and their perspective—now it's time to showcase their contributions. For example: *Bob gave me these forecasts and feels confident we'll hit the numbers.* If Bob is a superstar in his department, his endorsement will mean something. People who trust him will trust you.

Handle the Naysayers

Even the strongest business cases will get some pushback. Here are the most common types of resistance and tips on how to address them:

1. **"This is too good to be true."** Stakeholders may not believe that the benefits, sales, or savings you've identified are realistic. This happens in organizations where people frequently overpromise. If you think you'll face this roadblock, take extra care in backing up your numbers. For each benefit stream, identify a subject-matter expert who can credibly speak to the figure you've listed. If you're promising 25% sales growth, have your sales expert say how the team arrived at that estimate.

2. **"But you haven't thought of . . ."** Many stakeholders like to point out gaps: *You haven't even talked about how this will play out in Europe,*

and that's a critical region for us. They may also bring up risks that you didn't address in your presentation. Give honest, direct responses. If you haven't considered the issue, say so. Offer to look into it and get back to the committee. If you don't believe Europe is critical, you can ask the group whether they'd like you to do more research. If others agree with you, they may step in to say so.

3. **"We'll never get this done."** Another common concern is timing. Stakeholders may think you're being overly optimistic about when the project will be completed. Here, again, it's essential to have the support of those who will do the work. You can reply, "I've shared these timelines with IT and manufacturing, and they agree the work will take no longer than six months."

If people try to shoot down your case with objections like these, don't get defensive. Instead, "invite the lions in," as leadership and change expert John Kotter advises in his book *Buy-In*. When someone voices skepticism, thank him for his comment and engage him directly. Say something like, "Yes, I hear your concern. Let's go back to that issue and discuss how we're planning to address it." If you give a thorough, straightforward answer, chances are that your skeptic will back off—or people in the room will come to your defense. Invite your champion to comment if she can credibly address the concern.

End on a Positive Note

It's always a good sign when stakeholders say, "Tell me more." You know you're on the right track if they ask who would be assigned to the project or when you could get started. Whenever possible, close your presentation on a high note. Reiterate a positive NPV or highlight the significant need your project fills. No matter what questions arose during the discussion, you want stakeholders to remember the good your initiative will bring the company.

Chapter 16
Get to a Decision

After you've submitted or presented your case, you probably won't have to sit around biting your nails for long. Usually, decision makers respond either in the meeting itself or within a few days. You'll get one of four answers.

"No, the Project Isn't a Priority."

When cases get rejected, it's typically because they're not in sync with strategic goals, the ROI isn't high enough, or the organization simply doesn't have the funds or people to get it done. While this can be disappointing, keep in mind that "no" is sometimes the best answer for the business (as discussed in the introduction). Depending on the reason for the rejection, you may be able to build a stronger case later. If the project wasn't aligned closely enough with the company's objectives, you could propose it again when the goals evolve. Or you might collect information over the next year or so showing that the benefits are even stronger than you initially thought. Whether you plan to let your proposal go or revisit it in the next approval cycle, thank your champion, your subject-matter experts, and everyone else who helped you build the case. You might need their help later on.

"We Can't Make a Decision Yet."

Stakeholders who agree about the business need but don't think you've found the right solution may send you back to the drawing board. (This can also happen if you haven't told the story clearly or provided enough data.) Find out from your stakeholders what the sticking points are. Does the project take too long? Does it cost too much? Is a strategic element missing? In light of these concerns, revisit other alternatives that you and your team considered. Sometimes stakeholders already have another project in mind and your proposal just doesn't align with it. Have someone who's close to your stakeholders—whether it's your champion or a trusted subject-matter expert—work with them to understand more about the project they do want. Evaluate that idea and include it as one of the alternatives you come back with.

"We Can Approve Only Part of the Project."

Typically, there are two reasons why a review board will give you the go-ahead on just a portion of your case: process or issues.

On long projects or those with many risks, decision makers may hedge their bets and give you an OK to go up to some key milestone. Leaders at companies with this type of tollgate process intentionally fund only early stages so they can see if the assumptions are valid. The "yes" has a caveat—you'll need to reapply for funding for the next year or possibly even the next phase. This partial approval can be a blessing, since it gives you the opportunity to refine the solution as you move forward.

Sometimes review boards grant partial approval due to funding issues. It's not uncommon for a review committee to say that it can't greenlight your $2 million project, but it can give you part of that money. When that happens, you're expected to come back and explain what you can do with fewer resources.

The complexities surrounding partial approvals are discussed in chapter 17, "What Next?"

"Yes, Let's Move Ahead."

If you get a "yes," stakeholders will immediately start asking questions about resources: Who will lead the project (if not you)? How soon can you have a project plan in place? When can you pull together a team and get started on the work? Be ready with answers—you don't want to lose momentum after securing your hard-won approval.

A note of caution, though: "Yes" doesn't always mean yes. Conflict-averse leaders sometimes approve a project but then never allocate resources for it. If they withhold the dollars, people, and time it will take to do the work, they might as well have said no. You may be able to prevent this from happening by following up immediately with a detailed request for resources. Ask for the names of individuals assigned to the project. If managers won't give you names, they probably aren't assigning resources. In that case, ask your champion to talk with them and find out the reasons for the holdup—then address whatever concerns you can in the detailed project plan.

You can make a quick decision more likely by putting a time frame on your project. Explain that a window of opportunity will close if you don't move forward soon—perhaps it's an opening in the market because a competitor's product just flopped or the chance to upgrade an IT system during a facility upgrade. Don't be the boy who cried wolf, though. The urgency needs to be legitimate. Assuming it is, bringing this up in your presentation can help you get closure sooner rather than later.

No matter what the outcome of the decision, don't rest on your laurels. You can take steps forward whether your project was rejected or approved.

Chapter 17
What Next?

Whether you're popping a bottle of bubbly, walking despondently back to your desk, or pulling your hair out because you have to create and present a case all over again, remember that you've done your job—you've helped the company make a wise decision.

But the work is not over. If you got a yes, it's time to begin implementing your project. And even if the decision makers said no, there are steps you can and should take.

If You Heard "No, the Project Isn't a Priority."

First off, don't despair if your project isn't approved. Although it may feel like failure to hear "no," keep in mind that you've contributed to the success of the company by helping it identify that the project wasn't a worthwhile investment. The real purpose of a business case is not to necessarily win approval for your proposal, but to provide enough information so the committee can make an informed decision.

But don't just accept the "no" by saying thank you and walking away. Instead, always ask "Why?" If you know precisely why the decision makers rejected the case, then you'll be able to follow up appropriately. Ask this question in the meeting or in a subsequent email. Don't pick a fight or try to use the response to change the outcome, but seek to understand their reasoning. You might say, "Thanks for letting me know about your decision. I'd love any feedback you have on why the project wasn't approved."

The reviewers may have passed on your project for any of several reasons. For example, they might tell you that the project doesn't align with the company strategy. In this case, let it die. Any project that doesn't fit with the company's imperatives should be rejected.

If they thought the project wasn't viable—that the approach you described wouldn't yield the results you promised—you can go back and address their concerns. Do you need more data to show why the approach works? Can you create a prototype that will assuage their worries? You might ask for a small amount of funding to run a quick pilot to prove the project can succeed.

If the higher-ups say no because there aren't enough resources, hold on to your case in the event that resources become available. That actually happened to me at GE. Partway through the year, corporate decided to give our business unit some additional funding to invest in strategic product development projects. Some market dynamics had changed, making our market segments more attractive than others. The product manager and I quickly dusted off several business cases that had not been funded due to lack of resources during the previous year's strategic planning process. In less than a month, projects were approved and teams were getting down to work. Staying in close touch with your project champion so that she can keep you apprised of any changes will help you prepare for such opportunities.

When you ask for the reasons behind the rejection, you have to hope you'll get an honest answer. In most cases, you will. It may not be direct—the CEO may not say to you, "We didn't think you could pull off the project"—but you'll likely be able to infer the reasons. Try to read between the lines. If you're still not sure, ask the project champion for her insight. Whatever response you get, don't argue with the logic or take it personally. That's not a way to win allies—or support—for this or future projects.

If You Heard "We Can't Make a Decision Yet."

Having your proposal tabled is better than an outright "no," but it's still disappointing. In most cases, you'll just have to trust that you built and presented a solid case and then wait and see what happens. Any additional measures you take will depend on the decision makers' rationale. Typically, it's for one of three reasons.

The case hasn't made the first cut.

It could be that your case didn't make it into the "definite yes" pile. If the decision committee is reviewing multiple cases at once, it may divide proposals into yes, no, and maybe piles. At least you know your project is in the mix. There's no need to lobby for your case at this point, especially if your project champion is representing you to the decision makers.

The decision makers just haven't decided yet.

Sometimes you've got a management team full of ditherers who are unable or unwilling to make decisions on the spot. They might want to hold off until they're behind closed doors to make the final call. Of course, your project is more likely to be approved if your proposal clarifies what's in it for each of the decision makers. While you wait, though, you may want to periodically work through your champion to be sure your idea is still in front of people and to check if there's anyone else's ear you should get.

Sometimes, the committee hasn't decided because they're waiting for the outcome of another decision that has farther-reaching impact. This happened to me once, when a project I'd proposed was hanging in the balance while we waited to find out if an acquisition that was in the works would be successful. If the acquisition went through, our project wouldn't be needed. If the deal didn't go through, our project would help fill a larger product development void.

The strategy is on hold.

The third reason for tabling projects is that the strategy it supports is on hold or being reconceived. Use your internal network to stay abreast of where the strategy is going. Once you have that information, you'll have to tweak your case to reflect new goals, assumptions, or constraints. If your proposal focuses on U.S. customers, and your company has decided to focus more on European customers, for example, explore whether your idea could be carried out in the United Kingdom. Since you've done a good job preparing your business case, you'll easily be able to tweak it. This can be a great opportunity. Typically, senior leaders will want to do a project right away that aligns with the new imperatives to demonstrate support for the new strategy. With your carefully prepared plan, you could be first in line with a project that fits. Don't shoehorn your project into the new strategy, of course. If your case doesn't support it, don't make it.

Sometimes waiting for a final decision takes time—days, weeks, and even months. And the reason for the project—the pain point it's designed to address—likely isn't going away. There may not be a whole lot you can do, but look for opportunities to alleviate the pain a bit. If your case proposed a new system that would allow customer service representatives to respond more quickly to complaints, look for workarounds. Collaborate with the person heading up that department to see if he has any short-term ideas that will make things better.

While you're waiting, it's not a bad idea to find a simple, easy way to collect more information about the problem and its magnitude. Document what's happening so that when you have the opportunity to go back to the decision makers or to your project champion you can say, "This problem hasn't gone away; in fact, it's gotten worse." This will make your case stronger. If the problem is getting severe, you'll provide people with new information and change the story of your case: The boat's not just taking on water—it's sinking.

If You Heard "We Can Approve Only Part of the Project."

What if your case has three parts but the decision makers only approve one? Or they sign off on the first phase of your project but ask you to come back in six months or more to request the additional funding? This happens more often than people think. It's frustrating, but it doesn't have to demotivate you and your team. Instead, focus on the fact that the committee liked your idea and want to move it forward.

Chapter 16, "Get to a Decision," discussed how approval of just one part of your project is particularly common at companies that use a tollgate process. If this is the situation you're in, ask the review committee what risks or questions need to be resolved by the time you reach the first milestone. Then proceed as though your project will be fully funded. That will give you the best sense of whether the project will be a success. At the end of the funding period, be prepared to go back and explain which of your assumptions held true and which didn't. For instance, you might have determined that the product cost can be 10% less than planned or that the launch date will need to change by three months. Since you documented the source of all your original numbers and assumptions, it will be easy to check with those individuals for updates. Prepare to come back and present the business case again with updated information on the benefits or costs based on what you learned so far.

The most common scenario, however—and the most challenging—is when the decision makers come back and say, "OK, we know you wanted $2 million, but what can you do for $1 million?" When asked if you can do the project or reach the same goals with less time or money, never say yes right away. Instead, tell the reviewers that you'll get back to them—very quickly—so you have time to redo the business case with those new constraints.

When you commit to doing just part of the project, resist the temptation to overpromise. First, don't do an across-the-board cut. If the committee wants you to submit a proposal for a project that costs 30% less, don't try to do everything the original case did with 30% less resources. It's better to restructure the project completely. Ask yourself and your team: What is a viable business opportunity that we can fund with this much money to achieve a portion of the goal? Can we drop the European sales arm? Can we cut down the rollout time? Second, don't agree to a cut in resources without a cut in the benefits. This creates an almost impossible situation. If your original case promised $800,000 in revenue from the new product but now you're asked to cut the budget by 20%, chances are you won't be able to realize the full $800,000. You'll need to bring that number down as well. After all, if you don't have a full tank of gas, you can't go as far.

You'll be prepared for this conversation if you ran several scenarios in your spreadsheet (as described in chapter 7, "Consider Alternatives"). It's great if you have those numbers in your back pocket, but if not, go back and rerun your numbers. Fortunately, this is pretty easy because you've structured your spreadsheet well. Simply create another tab and change the relevant figures.

It's rare that a company can afford to fund every good idea. Instead of harping on the cuts you needed to make, focus your team on creating and implementing a new plan that will help pave the way for the rest of your project to be approved later on.

If You Heard "Yes, Let's Move Ahead."

First, celebrate. Open a bottle of champagne or take your team out for dinner. Then get to work. After all, the decision makers just opened a door and you've got to walk through it. You'll need to figure out how you transition from getting your project approved to implementing it.

Don't wait for the check. In most companies, a formal funding mechanism doesn't exist—nobody actually writes you a check. More likely you're told: OK, you've got the resources and people you need, get started.

After your celebration, the first step is to set up your project management process. Some companies have a methodology for this. If that's the case at your organization, reach out to your contact in the project planning or management group. This person can set you up with the appropriate tools, templates, checklists, or software to start the project.

If there isn't a formal process at your company, get the project moving yourself. Start by gathering your team and working on a project charter. Review the high-level implementation plan you outlined in the case and make sure it's still actionable. And keep the business case handy. It was the initial road map for the project and it will be helpful to refer to as you structure the work. See the *HBR Guide to Project Management* for more information on tools and templates to help you manage a project effectively.

You've succeeded in getting the organization behind your solution to an important business need, but this is just the beginning. Think of it as building a house: You've chosen the architect and the builders, you've agreed on a blueprint, the bank has approved the funding, and you have a rough schedule and budget—but you haven't broken ground yet. Now comes the real work.

Appendix A
Avoid Common Mistakes

When creating and pitching business cases, even experienced managers fall into these traps—but you can avoid them.

Mistake #1: Failing to Address the Company's Goals

Too many managers assume that the benefits of their proposed projects speak for themselves or are implicit in a strong ROI.

This often happens with IT initiatives. Take, for example, a project lead who wants to put in a new system because it's the industry standard and he fears the firm will fall behind the competition without it. He'll probably build a case demonstrating how the system will pay off in a few years. But how will it support the company's strategy? That's what senior leaders really want to know, because that's what they're on the hook to deliver. They won't approve anything that doesn't help them on that front. So when you're creating your case, show that you're meeting a clear business need that aligns with their goals.

Mistake #2: Ignoring Other Perspectives

Ideas rarely touch just one department—yet the people pitching them often fail to consider how they'll affect others in the organization.

Proposing a new product? It will be produced, marketed, and sold by colleagues in other functions, so you'll need their buy-in. Suppose the product makes three other lines obsolete: It's important to anticipate the impact on manufacturing processes, marketing, and sales projections. You can't just say, "Oh, and these three lines will go away."

Involve a cross-functional team when developing your case. Bring in experts whose departments will be affected by your idea. Share drafts of estimated costs and benefits with them, and ask if you've accurately gauged the impact on their teams. And think about your idea from their perspective: How will it benefit them? What will they need to contribute? What new work will they have to do? Include this information in your case—the review committee will expect it.

Mistake #3: Neglecting Transition Costs and Timing

Most managers realize they need to identify all the costs and benefits of a new system, facility, product, and so on—but they often don't factor in what it takes to make the switch.

Senior leaders need a handle on transition costs and how long it will take to fully realize benefits before they can decide whether to invest. Even if you can't give them exact figures, include rough estimates based on similar projects. This shows stakeholders that you're looking at the big picture and helps you gain support across the organization (see Mistake #2). If your colleagues in the quality department know you're asking for money to upgrade their systems and provide training for your product launch, for example, they're more likely to endorse your case. Amounts can be adjusted later on, when you have a better sense of the project's scope.

Mistake #4: Glossing Over Risks

The easiest way to poke holes in a business case is to ask, "What if?" I see executive teams do this all the time: "What if our competitors beat us to market? What happens to your projections then?" Or: "What if our key partner bails? What will it take to get a backup plan in place?" Unless you've adequately addressed things that could go wrong, your reviewers will surely ask about them.

It's not enough to throw in a brief nod to risks at the end of the presentation—or to say you'll examine them in the project's next phase. Executives want to see that you've thought through contingencies from the beginning. Of course, you can't account for every imaginable scenario, and stakeholders shouldn't expect you to. But look at the most likely possibilities, especially in light of recent business experience. For example, if the project will require you to outsource work, consider what happens if you can't find a qualified vendor or if your chosen vendor doesn't deliver on time.

It can be difficult to spot risks on your own, so appoint someone on your team to help you. As you're building your case, ask that person to challenge assumptions, to think like your stakeholders and raise the concerns they'll have. Or ask each member of your team to come up with five "What if?" questions. Encourage them to channel the approval committee when identifying risks. Does your CFO worry that the housing market will crash again? Is your division head preoccupied with a particular competitor? Those are the sorts of issues that will come up during review.

Mistake #5: Cluttering the Presentation with Jargon

Use plain language in your presentation so you won't bore and alienate your audience. The technical folks in the room will know what you mean by "backward compatibility" and "dual-layer technology," but others may not. People from several different functions will probably weigh in on your case, and if they can't understand it, you're in trouble. To avoid this problem, ask colleagues in other functions to review drafts, noting any opaque terms you should define or cut altogether.

In many firms, leaders review business cases on paper or on conference calls, so you may not get the chance to present face-to-face. Even if you do, you probably won't have time to give lengthy explanations—and your audience won't have the patience to listen to them. A clear, concise document always wins the day.

Appendix B
How to Give a
Killer Presentation

by Chris Anderson

Editor's note: Though giving a TED Talk to a large,
diverse audience is different from presenting a business case to the handful of stakeholders who will assess your project's value, this article provides helpful
tips on crafting and delivering your message.

A little more than a year ago, on a trip to Nairobi, Kenya,
some colleagues and I met a 12-year-old Masai boy
named Richard Turere, who told us a fascinating story. His
family raises livestock on the edge of a vast national park,
and one of the biggest challenges is protecting the ani-
mals from lions—especially at night. Richard had noticed

Reprinted from *Harvard Business Review,* June 2013 (product
#R1306K)

Find the perfect mix of data and narrative *by Nancy Duarte*

Most presentations lie somewhere on the continuum between a report and a story. A report is data-rich, exhaustive, and informative—but not very engaging. Stories help a speaker connect with an audience, but listeners often want facts and information, too. Great presenters layer story and information like a cake, and understand that different types of talks require differing ingredients.

Report
Literal,
Informational,
Factual,
Exhaustive

Story
Dramatic,
Experiential,
Evocative,
Persuasive

Research Findings
If your goal is to communicate information from a written report, send the full document to the audience in advance, and limit the presentation to key takeaways. Don't do a long slide show that repeats all your findings. Anyone who's really interested can read the report; everyone else will appreciate brevity.

Financial Presentation
Financial audiences love data, and they'll want the details. Satisfy their analytical appetite with facts, but add a thread of narrative to appeal to their emotional side. Then present the key takeaways visually, to help them find meaning in the numbers.

Product Launch
Instead of covering only specs and features, focus on the value your product brings to the world. Tell stories that show how real people will use it and why it will change their lives.

VC Pitch
For 30 minutes with a VC, prepare a crisp, well-structured story arc that conveys your idea compellingly in 10 minutes or less; then let Q&A drive the rest of the meeting. Anticipate questions and rehearse clear and concise answers.

Keynote Address
Formal talks at big events are high-stakes, high-impact opportunities to take your listeners on a transformative journey. Use a clear story framework and aim to engage them emotionally.

Nancy Duarte is the author of *HBR Guide to Persuasive Presentations*, *Slide:ology*, and *Resonate*. She is the CEO of Duarte, Inc., which designs presentations and teaches presentation development.

that placing lamps in a field didn't deter lion attacks, but when he walked the field with a torch, the lions stayed away. From a young age, he'd been interested in electronics, teaching himself by, for example, taking apart his parents' radio. He used that experience to devise a system of lights that would turn on and off in sequence—using solar panels, a car battery, and a motorcycle indicator box—and thereby create a sense of movement that he hoped would scare off the lions. He installed the lights, and the lions stopped attacking. Soon villages elsewhere in Kenya began installing Richard's "lion lights."

The story was inspiring and worthy of the broader audience that our TED conference could offer, but on the surface, Richard seemed an unlikely candidate to give a TED Talk. He was painfully shy. His English was halting. When he tried to describe his invention, the sentences tumbled out incoherently. And frankly, it was hard to imagine a preteenager standing on a stage in front of 1,400 people accustomed to hearing from polished speakers such as Bill Gates, Sir Ken Robinson, and Jill Bolte Taylor.

But Richard's story was so compelling that we invited him to speak. In the months before the 2013 conference, we worked with him to frame his story—to find the right place to begin, and to develop a succinct and logical arc of events. On the back of his invention, Richard had won a scholarship to one of Kenya's best schools, and there he had the chance to practice the talk several times in front of a live audience. It was critical that he build his confidence to the point where his personality could shine through. When he finally gave his talk at TED, in Long

Beach, you could tell he was nervous, but that only made him more engaging—people were hanging on his every word. The confidence was there, and every time Richard smiled, the audience melted. When he finished, the response was instantaneous: a sustained standing ovation. Since the first TED conference, 30 years ago, speakers have run the gamut from political figures, musicians, and TV personalities who are completely at ease before a crowd to lesser-known academics, scientists, and writers—some of whom feel deeply uncomfortable giving presentations. Over the years, we've sought to develop a process for helping inexperienced presenters to frame, practice, and deliver talks that people enjoy watching. It typically begins six to nine months before the event, and involves cycles of devising (and revising) a script, repeated rehearsals, and plenty of fine-tuning. We're continually tweaking our approach—because the art of public speaking is evolving in real time—but judging by public response, our basic regimen works well: Since we began putting TED Talks online, in 2006, they've been viewed more than one billion times.

On the basis of this experience, I'm convinced that giving a good talk is highly coachable. In a matter of hours, a speaker's content and delivery can be transformed from muddled to mesmerizing. And while my team's experience has focused on TED's 18-minutes-or-shorter format, the lessons we've learned are surely useful to other presenters—whether it's a CEO doing an IPO road show, a brand manager unveiling a new product, or a start-up pitching to VCs.

Frame Your Story

There's no way you can give a good talk unless you have something worth talking about. Conceptualizing and framing what you want to say is the most vital part of preparation.

We all know that humans are wired to listen to stories, and metaphors abound for the narrative structures that work best to engage people. When I think about compelling presentations, I think about taking an audience on a journey. A successful talk is a little miracle—people see the world differently afterward.

If you frame the talk as a journey, the biggest decisions are figuring out where to start and where to end. To find the right place to start, consider what people in the audience already know about your subject—and how much they care about it. If you assume they have more knowledge or interest than they do, or if you start using jargon or get too technical, you'll lose them. The most engaging speakers do a superb job of very quickly introducing the topic, explaining why they care so deeply about it, and convincing the audience members that they should, too.

The biggest problem I see in first drafts of presentations is that they try to cover too much ground. You can't summarize an entire career in a single talk. If you try to cram in everything you know, you won't have time to include key details, and your talk will disappear into abstract language that may make sense if your listeners are familiar with the subject matter but will be completely opaque if they're new to it. You need specific examples to flesh out your ideas. So limit the scope of your talk to that which can be explained, and brought to life with examples, in the available time. Much of the early feedback we give aims to correct the impulse to sweep too broadly. Instead, go deeper. Give more detail. Don't tell us about your entire field of study—tell us about your unique contribution.

Of course, it can be just as damaging to overexplain or painstakingly draw out the implications of a talk. And there the remedy is different: Remember that the people in the audience are intelligent. Let them figure some things out for themselves. Let them draw their own conclusions.

Many of the best talks have a narrative structure that loosely follows a detective story. The speaker starts out by presenting a problem and then describes the search for a solution. There's an "aha" moment, and the audience's perspective shifts in a meaningful way.

If a talk fails, it's almost always because the speaker didn't frame it correctly, misjudged the audience's level of interest, or neglected to tell a story. Even if the topic is important, random pontification without narrative is always deeply unsatisfying. There's no progression, and you don't feel that you're learning.

I was at an energy conference recently where two people—a city mayor and a former governor—gave back-to-back talks. The mayor's talk was essentially a list of impressive projects his city had undertaken. It came off as boasting, like a report card or an advertisement for his reelection. It quickly got boring. When the governor spoke, she didn't list achievements; instead, she shared an idea. Yes, she recounted anecdotes from her time in office, but the idea was central—and the stories explanatory or illustrative (and also funny). It was so much more interesting. The mayor's underlying point seemed to be how great he was, while the governor's message was "Here's a compelling idea that would benefit us all."

As a general rule, people are not very interested in talks about organizations or institutions (unless they're members of them). Ideas and stories fascinate us; organizations bore us—they're much harder to relate to. (Businesspeople especially take note: Don't boast about your company; rather, tell us about the problem you're solving.)

Plan Your Delivery

Once you've got the framing down, it's time to focus on your delivery. There are three main ways to deliver a talk. You can read it directly off a script or a teleprompter. You can develop a set of bullet points that map out what you're going to say in each section rather than scripting the whole thing word for word. Or you can memorize your talk, which entails rehearsing it to the point where you internalize every word—verbatim.

My advice: Don't read it, and don't use a teleprompter. It's usually just too distancing—people will know you're reading. And as soon as they sense it, the way they receive your talk will shift. Suddenly your intimate connection evaporates, and everything feels a lot more formal. We generally outlaw reading approaches of any kind at TED, though we made an exception a few years ago for a man who insisted on using a monitor. We set up a screen at the back of the auditorium, in the hope that the audience wouldn't notice it. At first he spoke naturally. But soon he stiffened up, and you could see this horrible sinking feeling pass through the audience as people realized, "Oh, no, he's reading to us!" The words were great, but the talk got poor ratings.

Obviously, not every presentation is worth that kind of investment of time. But if you do decide to memorize your talk, be aware that there's a predictable arc to the learning curve. Most people go through what I call the "valley of awkwardness," where they haven't quite memorized the talk. If they give the talk while stuck in that valley, the audience will sense it. Their words will sound recited, or there will be painful moments where they stare into the middle distance, or cast their eyes upward, as they struggle to remember their lines. This creates distance between the speaker and the audience.

Getting past this point is simple, fortunately. It's just a matter of rehearsing enough times that the flow of words becomes second nature. Then you can focus on delivering the talk with meaning and authenticity. Don't worry—you'll get there.

But if you don't have time to learn a speech thoroughly and get past that awkward valley, don't try. Go with bullet points on note cards. As long as you know what you want to say for each one, you'll be fine. Focus on remembering the transitions from one bullet point to the next.

Also pay attention to your tone. Some speakers may want to come across as authoritative or wise or powerful or passionate, but it's usually much better to just sound conversational. Don't force it. Don't orate. Just be you.

If a successful talk is a journey, make sure you don't start to annoy your travel companions along the way. Some speakers project too much ego. They sound condescending or full of themselves, and the audience shuts down. Don't let that happen.

Develop Stage Presence

For inexperienced speakers, the physical act of being on stage can be the most difficult part of giving a presentation—but people tend to overestimate its importance. Getting the words, story, and substance right is a much bigger determinant of success or failure than how you stand or whether you're visibly nervous. And when it comes to stage presence, a little coaching can go a long way.

The biggest mistake we see in early rehearsals is that people move their bodies too much. They sway from side to side, or shift their weight from one leg to the other. People do this naturally when they're nervous, but it's distracting and makes the speaker seem weak. Simply getting a person to keep his or her lower body motionless can dramatically improve stage presence. There are some people who are able to walk around a stage during a presentation, and that's fine if it comes naturally. But the vast majority are better off standing still and relying on hand gestures for emphasis.

Perhaps the most important physical act onstage is making eye contact. Find five or six friendly-looking people in different parts of the audience and look them in the eye as you speak. Think of them as friends you haven't seen in a year, whom you're bringing up to date on your work. That eye contact is incredibly powerful, and it will do more than anything else to help your talk land. Even if you don't have time to prepare fully and have to read from a script, looking up and making eye contact will make a huge difference.

Another big hurdle for inexperienced speakers is nervousness—both in advance of the talk and while they're onstage. People deal with this in different ways. Many speakers stay out in the audience until the moment they go on; this can work well, because keeping your mind engaged in the earlier speakers can distract you and limit nervousness. Amy Cuddy, a Harvard Business School professor who studies how certain body poses can affect power, utilized one of the more unusual preparation techniques I've seen. She recommends that people spend time before a talk striding around, standing tall, and extending their bodies; these poses make you feel more powerful. It's what she did before going onstage, and she delivered a phenomenal talk. But I think the single best advice is simply to breathe deeply before you go onstage. It works.

In general, people worry too much about nervousness. Nerves are not a disaster. The audience expects you to be nervous. It's a natural body response that can actually improve your performance: It gives you energy to perform and keeps your mind sharp. Just keep breathing, and you'll be fine.

Acknowledging nervousness can also create engagement. Showing your vulnerability, whether through nerves or tone of voice, is one of the most powerful ways to win over an audience, provided it is authentic. Susan

Cain, who wrote a book about introverts and spoke at our 2012 conference, was terrified about giving her talk. You could feel her fragility onstage, and it created this dynamic where the audience was rooting for her—everybody wanted to hug her afterward. The fact that we knew she was fighting to keep herself up there made it beautiful, and it was the most popular talk that year.

Many of our best and most popular TED Talks have been memorized word for word. If you're giving an important talk and you have the time to do this, it's the best way to go. But don't underestimate the work involved. One of our most memorable speakers was Jill Bolte Taylor, a brain researcher who had suffered a stroke. She talked about what she learned during the eight years it took her to recover. After crafting her story and undertaking many hours of solo practice, she rehearsed her talk dozens of times in front of an audience to be sure she had it down.

Plan the Multimedia

With so much technology at our disposal, it may feel almost mandatory to use, at a minimum, presentation slides. By now most people have heard the advice about PowerPoint: Keep it simple; don't use a slide deck as a substitute for notes (by, say, listing the bullet points you'll discuss—those are best put on note cards); and don't repeat out loud words that are on the slide. Not only is reciting slides a variation of the teleprompter problem—"Oh, no, she's reading to us, too!"—but information is interesting only once, and hearing and seeing the same words feels repetitive. That advice may seem universal by now, but go into any company and you'll see presenters violating it every day.

Many of the best TED speakers don't use slides at all, and many talks don't require them. If you have photographs or illustrations that make the topic come alive, then yes, show them. If not, consider doing without, at least for some parts of the presentation. And if you're going to use slides, it's worth exploring alternatives to PowerPoint. For instance, TED has invested in the company Prezi, which makes presentation software that offers a camera's-eye view of a two-dimensional landscape. Instead of a flat sequence of images, you can move around the landscape and zoom in to it if need be. Used properly, such techniques can dramatically boost the visual punch of a talk and enhance its meaning.

Artists, architects, photographers, and designers have the best opportunity to use visuals. Slides can help frame and pace a talk and help speakers avoid getting lost in jargon or overly intellectual language. (Art can be hard to talk about—better to experience it visually.) I've seen great presentations in which the artist or designer put slides on an automatic timer so that the image changed every 15 seconds. I've also seen presenters give a talk accompanied by video, speaking along to it. That can help sustain momentum. The industrial designer Ross Lovegrove's highly visual TED Talk, for instance, used this technique to bring the audience along on a remarkable creative journey.

Another approach creative types might consider is to build silence into their talks, and just let the work speak for itself. The kinetic sculptor Reuben Margolin used that approach to powerful effect. The idea is not to think

"I'm giving a talk." Instead, think "I want to give this au- dience a powerful experience of my work." The single worst thing artists and architects can do is to retreat into abstract or conceptual language.

Video has obvious uses for many speakers. In a TED Talk about the intelligence of crows, for instance, the sci- entist showed a clip of a crow bending a hook to fish a piece of food out of a tube—essentially creating a tool. It illustrated his point far better than anything he could have said.

Used well, video can be very effective, but there are common mistakes that should be avoided. A clip needs to be short—if it's more than 60 seconds, you risk los- ing people. Don't use videos—particularly corporate ones—that sound self-promotional or like infomercials; people are conditioned to tune those out. Anything with a soundtrack can be dangerously off-putting. And what- ever you do, don't show a clip of yourself being inter- viewed on, say, CNN. I've seen speakers do this, and it's a really bad idea—no one wants to go along with you on your ego trip. The people in your audience are already listening to you live; why would they want to simultane- ously watch your talking-head clip on a screen?

Putting It Together

We start helping speakers prepare their talks six months (or more) in advance so that they'll have plenty of time to practice. We want people's talks to be in final form at least a month before the event. The more practice they can do in the final weeks, the better off they'll be. Ideally, they'll practice the talk on their own and in front of an audience.

The tricky part about rehearsing a presentation in front of other people is that they will feel obligated to offer feedback and constructive criticism. Often the feedback from different people will vary or directly conflict. This can be confusing or even paralyzing, which is why it's important to be choosy about the people you use as a test audience and whom you invite to offer feedback. In general, the more experience a person has as a presenter, the better the criticism he or she can offer.

I learned many of these lessons myself in 2011. My colleague Bruno Giussani, who curates our TEDGlobal event, pointed out that although I'd worked at TED for nine years, served as the emcee at our conferences, and introduced many of the speakers, I'd never actually given a TED Talk myself. So he invited me to give one, and I accepted.

It was more stressful than I'd expected. Even though I spend time helping others frame their stories, framing my own in a way that felt compelling was difficult. I decided to memorize my presentation, which was about how web video powers global innovation, and that was really hard: Even though I was putting in a lot of hours and getting sound advice from my colleagues, I definitely hit a point where I didn't quite have it down and began to doubt I ever would. I really thought I might bomb. I was nervous right up until the moment I took the stage. But it ended up going fine. It's definitely not one of the all-time great TED Talks, but it got a positive reaction—and I survived the stress of going through it.

Ultimately, I learned firsthand what our speakers have been discovering for three decades: Presentations rise or fall on the quality of the idea, the narrative, and the passion of the speaker. It's about substance, not speaking style or multimedia pyrotechnics. It's fairly easy to "coach out" the problems in a talk, but there's no way to "coach in" the basic story—the presenter has to have the raw material. If you have something to say, you can build a great talk. But if the central theme isn't there, you're better off not speaking. Decline the invitation. Go back to work and wait until you have a compelling idea that's really worth sharing.

The single most important thing to remember is that there is no one good way to do a talk. The most memorable talks offer something fresh, something no one has seen before. The worst ones are those that feel formulaic. So do not on any account try to emulate every piece of advice I've offered here. Take the bulk of it on board, sure. But make the talk your own. You know what's distinctive about you and your idea. Play to your strengths and give a talk that is truly authentic to you.

———

Chris Anderson is the curator of TED.

Glossary

Beneficiaries. Those inside or outside the organization who stand to gain from the project or initiative you are proposing.

Break-Even Point. Method of calculating ROI that determines how many units you need to sell in order to pay for the project.

Capital Expenditures. Money spent to acquire or develop an asset—which then depreciates, or decreases in value, over its life.

Internal Rate of Return (IRR). Method of calculating ROI that shows a project's investment value—essentially, the percentage of return you would get by investing the same amount of money in a CD that performed equally well.

Net Present Value (NPV). Method of calculating ROI that expresses the value of a long-term investment in today's dollars.

Operating Costs. Amount of money it will take to maintain the result of the project you are proposing. Includes ongoing expenses and overhead such as personnel, office space, and maintenance and licensing fees.

Payback Period. Method of calculating ROI that shows how many months or years it will take to earn back the money invested.

Productivity Savings. Costs you avoid through greater efficiency. Achieved either by changing the product cost baseline (with less-expensive materials, for example) or by cutting overhead costs (ongoing expenses that stem from how you run the business).

Project Expenditures. Onetime costs of doing the upfront project work, such as development, testing, training and deployment, and travel.

Proof of Concept. A small pilot project that tests your hypothesis about the business need for a project before you develop and present a solution.

Return on Investment (ROI). An estimate of the project's value. Four ROI measures calculated by using a stream of costs and benefits over time: break-even point, payback period, net present value, and internal rate of return.

Revenue. Money brought into the organization through sales.

Stakeholders. People with the authority to approve or reject your business case.

Sunk Costs. Money your organization has already spent on a project and will never get back.

Tollgate Process. Multiphased project approval, allowing stakeholders to decide one phase at a time whether to commit resources.

Index

alternative options and solutions,
    37–41, 100
assumptions, checking, 80, 84.
    See also risks
audience
    decision makers, 8, 13–15, 17,
        20–21, 105–117
    objectives of, 13, 17–21
    See also stakeholders

benchmarking, 59. *See also* un-
    certainty, managing
beneficiaries
    consulting with, 26–27, 44–45
    cross-functional teams and,
        33, 34
    definition of, 139
    identifying, 4
    involving in discussion, 100
    See also stakeholders; cross-
        functional teams
benefits
    estimating, 5, 49–60
    intangible, 55
    productivity savings, 53, 54–55
    revenue, 53–54
    tracking, 58–59
    types of, 53–55
brainstorming options (or alter-
    natives), 37–41
break-even analysis, 63, 64–66,
    139. *See also* ROI

business case
    accounting for risks in, 79–84
    basics of making, 3–6
    competition and, 95–96
    decisions about, 105–117
    document preparation for,
        87–92
    evaluation of, 7–10, 77
    financials for, 49–77
    getting feedback on, 93–96
    goal for, xi–xii
    high-level project plan for,
        43–46
    making pitch for, 99–103
    mistakes to avoid, 119–122
    need for clarification in, 25–32
    presentation of (*see*
        presentations)
    reasons for developing, xii–xiii
    rejection of, 105–106, 109–111
    structure of, 89, 91–92
    templates for, 88
business need
    clarifying, 25–32
    developing solutions for,
        29–31, 37–41
    documentation and, 31–32
    identifying, 3–5
    presenting, 89
    starting with, in presentation,
        99
business priorities, 17–21
business strategy, 19

capital expenditures, 51–52, 139.
See also costs
cash flows, 50–51, 67, 70
champion, project, 14–15, 20,
40, 93, 112–114. See also
stakeholders
closing slide of business case, 91.
See also presentations
company goals, 17–21, 119–120.
See also mistakes to avoid
competition, of other cases,
95–96
cost of goods sold (COGS),
53–54. See also costs
costs
capital expenditures, 51–52
estimating, 5, 49–60
intangible, 55
operating, 52, 54–55
personnel, 54
project, 51–52
sunk, 60
tracking, 58–59
transition, 43–44, 52–53,
120–121
types of, 51–53
cross-functional teams, 20–21,
33–36, 120
customers, 34–35. See also cross-
functional teams

decision makers
gathering information about,
20–21
identifying, 13–15
interests of, 17–21
lack of decision by, 106,
111–114
reaching out to, 8
responses by, 105–117
decisions, 105–117
approvals, 107–108, 116–117
lack of, 106, 111–114
negative, 105–106, 109–111
partial approvals, 106–107,
114–116
delivery, planning, for presentations, 129–131

depreciation, 51–52. See also
costs
discount rate, for NPV, 72, 73, 74
documentation, 31–32, 113
document preparation, 87–92.
See also presentations
dominant departments, 14. See
also stakeholders
do-nothing option, 39–40

evaluation process, 7–10
executive summary, 89, 90–91,
92
experts
cross-functional, 20–21, 120
external, 35. See also cross-
functional teams
financial information from,
55–58
highlighting, in presentations,
101
subject-matter, 4, 33, 40–41,
44, 79, 94, 101

facility investments, xii–xiii,
25, 89
finance department, 57–58
finance representative, 34. See
also cross-functional teams
financials
accounting for risks, 79–84
estimating costs and benefits,
49–60
forecasts, 56–57
gut-checking, 79–82
managing uncertainty about,
59–60
negative or low numbers, 75,
77
presenting, 91
return on investment (ROI), 5,
52, 61–77. See also break-
even analysis; payback
period; net present value;
internal rate of return
sources of information for,
55–58

testing the numbers, 82–84
tracking, 58–59
forecasts, 56–57

goals, company, 17–21, 119–120

high-level plan, 5, 43–46

income statement, 50. *See also*
    costs
information
    from beneficiaries, 26–27
    on financials, 55–58
    gathering, about stakeholders,
        20–21
intangible benefits, 55. *See also*
    costs
intangible costs, 55. *See also* costs
internal rate of return (IRR), 63,
    64, 74–75, 139. *See also* ROI
investors
    IRR and, 74–75
    understanding objectives
        of, 18

mistakes to avoid, 119–122
money, time value of, 71. *See also*
    net present value
multimedia presentations, 133–
    135. *See also* presentations

narrative structure, for presenta-
    tions, 124, 127–129. *See also*
    presentations
naysayers, 101–102. *See also*
    presentations
negative returns, 75, 77. *See also*
    ROI
nervousness, during presenta-
    tions, 132–133. *See also*
    presentations
net present value (NPV), 63, 64,
    71–74, 75, 77, 139. *See also*
    ROI

objections, handling, 101–102.
    See also presentations
opening slide of business
    case, 89, 92. *See also*
    presentations
operating costs, 52, 54–55, 140.
    See also costs
opportunity assessment, 81. *See
    also* risks

partial approvals, 106–107,
    114–116
payback period, 63, 64, 66–71,
    140. *See also* ROI
personal network, 15, 56
personnel costs, 54. *See also* costs
personnel factors, and assump-
    tions, 80. *See also* risks
perspectives, ignoring other, 120.
    See also mistakes to avoid
pilot projects, 30–31, 110
PowerPoint tips, 133–134. *See
    also* presentations
presentations
    brevity in, 99–100
    checklist for, 97–98
    clarity in, 5
    data and narrative mix in, 124
    delivery, planning for, 129–131
    document preparation for,
        87–92
    ending on positive note in,
        103
    framing story in, 127–129
    handling naysayers during,
        101–102
    jargon in, 122. *See also* mis-
        takes to avoid
    looking at past in, 88–89
    making pitch in, 99–103
    multimedia for, 133–135
    personalizing, 100
    preparation for, 135–137
    stage presence and, 131–133
    starting with the business
        need in, 99
    structure for, 89, 91–92
    tips for, 123–137

problems
    analyzing, 27–29
    developing solutions for,
        29–31
    identifying, 25–27
process-flow analysis, 27–29
productivity savings, 53, 54–55,
    140
project champion, 14–15, 20,
    40, 93, 112–114. *See also*
    stakeholders
project costs, 51–52. *See also*
    costs
project overview, in business
    case, 89
projects
    approval of, 107–108, 116–117
    funding of, 114–115
    high-level view of, 5, 43–46
    implementing, 116–117
    lack of approval for, 105–106,
        109–111
    lack of decision about, 106,
        111–114
    next steps for, 109–117
    partial approval of, 106–107,
        114–116
    plan, 43–46

quality, and assumptions, 80, 95.
    See also risks

rejections, 105–106, 109–111
return on investment (ROI), 5,
    52, 61–77, 79, 99, 140. *See
    also* break-even analysis;
    payback period; net pres-
    ent value; internal rate of
    return
revenue, 53–54, 140
review committee, 15, 94–95,
    107. *See also* stakeholders
risks
    accounting for, 79–84
    glossing over, 121–122. *See also*
    mistakes to avoid

identified by stakeholders,
    101–102
presenting, 91, 100
ROI. *See* return on investment
    (ROI)

schedule, 81, 91
scope, and assumptions, 80–81.
    See also risks
slides, 133–134. *See also*
    presentations
solutions
    alternative, 37–41, 100
    do-nothing option, 39–40
    narrowing down possible,
        40–41
spreadsheets
    break-even, 62
    factoring risks into, 83
    internal rate of return (IRR),
        75, 76
    net present value (NPV),
        72–73
    payback period, 67–70
    return on investment (ROI),
        61–62
    tracking financials in, 58–59
stage presence, 131–133. *See also*
    presentations
stakeholders
    buy-in from, 93–96
    concerns of, 81–82, 95
    decisions by, 105–108
    definition of, 141
    gathering information about,
        20–21
    identifying, 4
    involving in discussion, 100
    meeting with, 94
    perspectives of, 120
    presentations to, 87–88
    resistance from, 101–102
    solution development and,
        29–30
    support from, 35, 57
    track record of, 21
start-ups, pitching, xi–xii

stealth projects, 30–31
story framing, 3–6, 127–129. *See also* presentations
strategic goals, 17–21
structured argument, 89, 91–92
subject-matter experts, 4, 33, 40–41, 44, 79, 94, 101
sunk costs, 60, 141. *See also* costs

teams
    consulting, 44–45
    cross-functional, 20–21, 33–36, 120
technology
    and assumptions, 80. *See also* risks
    and presentations, 133–135. *See also* presentations
templates, for business case. *See* business case, structure of
threat assessment, 81. *See also* risks
time value of money, 71. *See also* net present value
timing, 102, 120–121. *See also* mistakes to avoid
tollgate process, 9, 106–107, 114, 141
transition costs, 43–44, 52–53, 120–121. *See also* costs; mistakes to avoid

uncertainty, managing, 59–60. *See also* costs

About the Authors

Raymond Sheen, PMP, is the president of Product & Process Innovation, a consulting firm specializing in project management, product development, and process improvement. He teaches seminars on developing and reviewing business cases at Worcester Polytechnic Institute, Clemson University, and the China Institute for Innovation. Sheen has managed projects for both government and private organizations. He prepared and reviewed hundreds of business cases when he worked at General Electric—both as a member of corporate staff and as an engineering executive within GE's Industrial Systems business. He holds engineering degrees from the U.S. Air Force Academy and the Massachusetts Institute of Technology. He and his family reside in South Carolina.

Amy Gallo is a contributing editor at *Harvard Business Review* and is the author of the forthcoming *HBR Guide to Managing Conflict at Work*. Her writing appears regularly on HBR.org. Before working as a writer and editor, she was a consultant at Katzenbach Partners, a strategy and organization consulting firm based in New York.

Notes

Notes

Notes

Notes

Notes

Notes

Notes

Notes

Business Case

Now that you have completed the *HBR Guide to Building Your Business Case*, how can you ensure your next case gets the green light?

The **HBR Guide to Building Your Business Case Ebook + Tools** delivers a set of helpful directions, references, and templates to help you develop and execute a successful business case. We've done the work for you with a series of ready-to-use digital tools, including:

→ Customizable business case and ROI templates

→ Several methods for determining ROI (breakeven, payback, net present value, internal rate of return)

→ Two annotated sample business cases with ROI worksheets

Ensure your next business case is a success with the *HBR Guide to Building Your Business Case Ebook + Tools*, available exclusively at hbr.org for just $39.95.

Smart advice and inspiration from a source you trust.

Harvard Business Review Guides

Packed with concise, practical tips from leading experts—and examples that make them easy to apply—the HBR Guides series provides smart answers to your most pressing work challenges. Arm yourself with the advice you need to succeed on the job, from the most trusted brand in business.

AVAILABLE IN PAPERBACK
OR EBOOK FORMAT
WHEREVER BOOKS ARE SOLD

- Better Business Writing
- Coaching Employees
- Finance Basics for Managers
- Getting the Mentoring You Need
- Getting the Right Work Done

- Managing Stress at Work
- Managing Up and Across
- Office Politics
- Persuasive Presentations
- Project Management

BUY FOR YOUR TEAM, COMPANY, OR EVENT.
To learn more about bulk discounts visit hbr.org.